Canoeing and Camping
Beyond the Basics

by Cliff Jacobson

Illustrations by Cliff Moen

ICS BOOKS, Inc.
Merrillville, Indiana

CANOEING AND CAMPING, BEYOND THE BASICS

Printed in U.S.A.

DEDICATION

To Susie, whose dreams take her beyond the beaten path.

ACKNOWLEDGMENTS

A special thanks to Cliff Moen, Harry Roberts, Phil Sigglekow, Dr. Bill Forgey, and my publisher, Tom Todd. Thanks also to *Canoe* magazine, *Canoesport Journal*, and *Boat Pennsylvania* magazine for permission to use portions of my articles that have appeared in these publications.

Published by:
ICS Books, Inc.
1370 E. 86th Place
Merrillville, IN   46410
800–541–7323

LIBRARY OF CONGRESS CATALOGING-IN-PUBLICATION DATA

Jacobson, Cliff.
    Canoeing and camping : beyond the basics / Cliff Jacobson ;
illustrations by Cliff Moen.
        p.   cm.
    Includes index.
    ISBN 0-934802-80-7 : $9.99
    1. Canoes and canoeing. 2. Camping.   I. Title.
GV790.J33 1992
797.1'22--dc20   92-4582
                                                       CIP

TABLE OF CONTENTS

Part 1 Equipment

Part II Canoe Skills

Part III Applied Skills

Part IV Camping Skills

PART ONE

Equipment

CHAPTER ONE

The Wilderness Canoe - an Investment in Freedom

M y love affair with canoeing began in 1966 when a friend invited me to join him on a float trip down a small Indiana stream. It sounded like fun and rekindled memories of the good times I'd had on trips taken as a Boy Scout. It was a glorious day for a river float: warm, bright, and with a persistent breeze. The river was pleasant but not spectacular and the canoe was a badly made fiberglass model that weighed at least ninety pounds. But no matter—the gentle beauty of the experience captured my heart. From then on I vowed to never be without a canoe of some sort.

Within the year I purchased my first canoe: a fifteen-foot fiberglass cheapie very much like my friend's. I pinched pennies for months to buy that boat and was very paranoid about the possibility that it might be stolen. So when I camped out, I confidently chained it to a tree or the doors of my car!

I paddled that canoe in blissful ignorance for more than a year before I purchased my first high-performance boat: a 17-foot-9-inch Sawyer Cruiser. After that, came three aluminum Grummans of various lengths and weights, another Sawyer, six Old Towns, five Mad Rivers, three Daggers, one Bell, and three cedarstrip canoes that I built myself. Ultimately I ran out of storage room in my garage and was forced to sell some off—a terribly painful experience for someone who loves canoes as much as I do. Fortunately, I now own two canoe trailers, so the possibility of adding to my ten canoes excites me.

As you can see, canoe fever is incurable. One remedy is to simply paddle at every opportunity. Mill ponds, lazy rivers, wilderness lakes—it makes no difference. That's the beauty of the canoe: it's the only craft I know that is as much at home on tiny creeks as it is on giant lakes and reservoirs. I've even paddled mine on the ocean with complete confidence!

SELECTING THE WILDERNESS CANOE

Wilderness canoes should be longer and deeper than those used for day tripping. Long canoes are faster (and thus easier to paddle) than short canoes, and deep hulls provide a margin of safety on windlashed lakes and thrashing rapids. Choose a canoe at least 17 feet long, with a width (beam) of not less than 34 inches and a center depth of at least 13 ½ inches. The bows should have increasing flare so they'll have sufficient buoyancy to climb up over big waves without knifing dangerously through them.

Because a canoe's ability to rise and fall easily with the waves depends upon its hull design and not the height of its ends, high bows and sterns serve little purpose other than to add weight to the canoe. Generally, ends should not be higher than the center depth of the canoe plus 10 inches. Thus, a canoe with a 13-inch depth should have a maximum end height of 23 inches. Ends that are too high act as sails, making canoe-handling on windblown lakes difficult.

KEELS: FRIEND'S OR FIEND'S?

An external keel will make any canoe track (hold its course) better. However, it will also act as a cow-catcher in rapids: it will hang up on rocks and cause upsets. There's smug satisfaction in watching your friends spill when the keel of their canoe catches on the same rock that your keelless canoe easily slid over just moments before. Later, when your friends have dried out, you'll swear that your superiority in rapids is due to your impeccable paddling skill rather than to a smoothbottomed canoe!

Let's not mince words. External keels are generally the sign of an inferior canoe design. A canoe that requires an afterthought tacked on below to make it paddle straight belongs back on the redrawing board. Good tracking may be achieved simply by combining a round or V bottom, narrow ends, a straight keel line (see the section on rocker below), and somewhat squarish stems (ends). Aluminum canoes are formed in two halves, so they need a keel to hold the halves together. But even here the keel could be mounted on the inside of the hull rather than the outside.

The real reason for keels is to stiffen a floppy bottom. The biggest, flattest canoe bottom can be strengthened considerably by hanging a piece of angle aluminum or a one-by-two along its length. Throw in a bunch of ribs and maybe a vertical strut or three, and the most shapeless hull will become rigid.

My recommendation: Avoid canoes with keels. The exceptions are aluminum canoes, which don't come any other way. Some aluminum canoe makers offer shallow-draft "shoe" keels on their heavyweight whitewater models. Shoe keels make a lot more sense than the standard T-grip rock grabbers.

ROCKER

The fore and aft upward curve of the keelline of a canoe is called rocker. A canoe with lots of rocker (1½ inches is a lot) will turn easily in rapids and rise quickly to oncoming waves. But it will track poorly and be slower on the flats than a similar hull with no rocker.

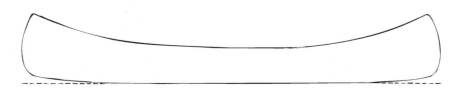

Figure 1-1 The fore and aft upward curve of the keelline of a canoe called "rocker." Rockered canoes turn more easily than those without rocker.

Racers like a canoe with zero rocker—perhaps a hint of lift in the ends, that's all. Whitewater canoes should have severe rocker—3 or more inches is not uncommon. A wilderness tripper might fall somewhere in between—about 1 to one 1½ inches. The important thing to consider is how the boat will be used. A canoe that tracks like a mountain cat when near empty will turn even more reluctantly when heavily loaded. A heavy load forces a canoe down into the water (acts like a keel) and so improves tracking. Wilderness canoes ordinarily are heavily loaded and therefore require some rocker. Conversely, it makes little sense to have lots of rocker in a minimally loaded day cruiser.

The amount of rocker a canoe needs depends largely on its length and hull configuration. Short hulls need less rocker than long ones, and flat-bottomed canoes turn more easily than round-bottomed ones. Very short canoes—14½ feet or less (solo boats)—with no rocker may be turned easily with minimal paddle effort by simply leaning them on their sides (you use the rocker in the sidewall). A rocker of more than one 1½ inches is ridiculous in a true solo canoe unless, of course, it's a flat out whitewater slalom boat.

My advice: Use a tape measure to determine the amount of rocker in a canoe before you buy it. Figure on zero rocker for a racer, maybe a ½ inch for a day cruiser, and up to 1½ inches for a wilderness tripper. For all out whitewater use, the more rocker the merrier.

TUMBLEHOME

The inward curve of the sides of a canoe *above the waterline* is called tumblehome. Some canoes have lots of tumblehome; others have none at all. Tumblehome is used for the following reasons.

The craft can be made wide at the waterline for stability and narrow at the gunwales for ease of paddling (you don't have to reach so far over the side).

Curved sidewalls are more rigid than broad, flat areas; thus a canoe with lots of tumblehome will be stiffer and require less bracing than a gently arched or radically flared boat.

The most seaworthy configuration of any watercraft consists of sides that flare boldly right to the gunwales, such as in a wild-river dory. Nonetheless, most of the best tripping canoes necessarily feature some tumblehome to maintain

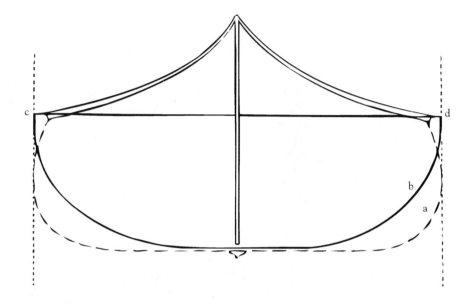

Figure 1-2 The inward curve of the sides of the canoe above the waterline is called "tumblehome" (canoe "a"). Canoe "b" has flared sides which are much more seaworthy. Note that the maximum beam (c–d) is the same for both canoes.

sidewall stiffness and reduce gunwale width. Given a choice, I'd choose a canoe with no tumblehome whatsoever. Unfortunately, a lot of very good canoes don't come this way. Moral? Moderation in all things. It couldn't be more true for that ol'debbil tumblehome!

FLAT OR ROUND BOTTOM?
Virtually every text on wilderness canoeing recommends flat-bottomed canoes over round-bottomed ones on the assumption that round-bottomed hulls lack stability. Yet the fact remains that accomplished canoeists prefer round-or, yes, v-bottomed canoes for use on every type of water, from placid lakes to thundering rapids.

As far as stability is concerned, when it is loaded, a round-bottomed canoe feels nearly as stable as a flat-bottomed one, and in reality the round hull is far more stable in rough water because you can control the canoe with your body. The responsiveness of the round hull permits you to make small balance adjustments easily. You can ride the waves and rapids and feel every movement of the canoe—like a jockey on a well-trained racehorse. Should you broach (turn broadside to the waves), you can immediately transfer your weight to expose more of the side of the canoe to the oncoming waves. On the other hand, the sluggishness of a flat-bottomed canoe prevents much real control except for steering.

Because of their curved shape, round bottoms are stronger than flat bottoms. Thus, round-bottomed canoes do not usually require the additional reinforcement of keels. Keelless, flat-bottomed canoes commonly suffer from lack of hull rigidity and have difficulty retaining their bottom shape when paddled through the water.

Additionally, round-bottomed hulls are considerably faster than flat-bottomed ones. Although you may not be concerned with speed, the time may come when you will need to paddle many miles against the wind on a large lake. At this time you will be grateful for whatever speed your canoe possesses.

Selecting a Store Bought Canoe

Since you usually can't take a new canoe out and try it before you buy, here are some things to look for and some tests to perform right in the store:

1. Use a tape measure to determine length, width, and depth. Don't believe the manufacturer's specifications. Is the canoe big enough for rough water?
2. Place the canoe on grass, a carpet, or the showroom floor. Climb in. Can you kneel beneath each seat? This is important because kneeling increases stability, and you'll often find it necessary to kneel in the rough water of rapids. Exception: Some finelined canoes are so narrow in the bow that kneeling is impractical (you can't spread you knees wide for stability). In these boats it's better to have a low-mounted seat and to brace your feet solidly against the bow flotation tank or an improvised footbrace of some sort.
3. The manufacturer's listed canoe weights are almost always overoptimistic (I have never owned a canoe that weighed less than its advertised weight). Take a bathroom scale with you when you go canoeshopping!
4. Spin the canoe around on the ground. If it spins easily and is a keelless model, it probably has a fair amount of rocker and will turn easily. You can also look at the hull at ground level to see how much dead rise there is at the ends; or you can measure it precisely. But the spin test will approximate maneuverability if you compare several canoe models. Remember, you want a canoe that turns reasonably well when loaded.
5. You will probably carry a wilderness canoe almost as much as you will paddle it. The carrying yoke or center thwart should be installed almost at the exact center of the canoe. Have the salesperson help you place the canoe on your shoulders (just let the center thwart rest on your neck). Is the canoe balanced, or is one end much heavier than the other? If the canoe is out of balance, can the center thwart be easily moved?

6. Canoes built of nonbuoyant materials must have built-in flotation Usually, this consists of Styrofoam blocks placed in sealed compartments at each end of the canoe. Make sure flotation does not interfere with front leg room.

7. To prevent bottom wobble, flat-bottomed canoes should have an inner or outer keel, or they should have their bottoms reinforced with additional material.

As you look around for the ideal wilderness canoe, remember that most novice canoeists buy small, short canoes because they are light and easy to handle and store. As a result, many manufacturers design their small canoes for an inexperienced market, with high bows and sterns, plastic gunwales, flotation under the seats, big keels, and so on. Experienced canoeists usually select the longest and deepest canoes they can carry; thus, big canoes are usually designed to meet the needs of more knowledgeable paddlers.

THE CASE FOR THE SHORT CANOE

If your canoeing will be limited to the near wilderness of small streams and rivers, a small, light canoe may be right for you. If you plan to do a lot of rock dodging in shallow rapids or to twist your way down narrow, mountain fed streams like the ones in North Carolina, Vermont, and West Virginia, a 16-foot, deep-hulled canoe would be a good choice. Short canoes generally turn quickly and are light and easy to handle on portages.

Carrying long canoes through brushy areas, between trees, and up and down steep banks can be very frustrating. It is in these areas that the short canoe excels. And if you prefer to paddle alone (see chapter II, Solo Canoeing Is Different), you will find a lightly loaded, narrow, 14- to 16-foot canoe to be fast, responsive, and easily maneuvered.

Tandem (two person) canoes that are shorter than 16 feet, however, respond sluggishly to the paddle and have poor directional stability. With the exception of specialized whitewater craft, such canoes are better adapted to portaging than paddling. There is little sense in buying, paddling, or carrying more canoe than you need. However, to attempt a rough-water voyage with a canoe that is too small is to invite disaster!

NEW CANOE DESIGNS

One of the most exciting improvements in canoe design has been the appearance of the asymmetric hull. Basically, this consists of a long, narrow, somewhat flared bow with a fairly uniform taper and a fat, buoyant stern. By placing the maximum beam (width) of the canoe behind center, the bow presents a finer entry (narrower wedge) to the water. The result is a canoe that is faster on all types of water.

Virtually all competitive racing canoes are asymmetric, as are most of the best high-performance cruisers. There's no denying the advantages of asymmetry for straight-ahead running, even in big brawny rapids. But *very* asymmetric hulls may be unpredictable in tricky currents and when performing precise slalom

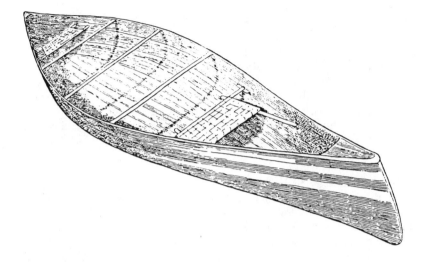

Figure 1-3 An Asymmetric Canoe: There's no denying the advantages of asymmetry for straight-ahead running, but asymmetric canoes are often unpredictable in tricky currents.

maneuvers that require strong leans. For this reason I prefer symmetrical—or nearly symmetrical—boats for all-round wilderness travel where a variety of water conditions will be encountered.

FREEBOARD

Freeboard is the distance from the waterline to the top of the gunwales at their lowest point. The greater the freeboard, the greater the ability of the canoe to handle rough water, assuming the canoe is well designed.

While some experts recommend a minimum of 6 inches of freeboard, no serious canoeist I know would think of using any canoe so heavily loaded on any but a mirror-calm lake. My own preference is a 9-inch minimum. A deep-hulled 17- to 18-foot canoe will easily ride that high if moderately loaded.

WEIGHT

Portaging is part of the daily routine in wilderness travel, so select a canoe you can carry long distances; then, learn to paddle it well. Fifty-five to seventy pounds is a reasonable weight for a high- volume, durable, tripping canoe that will be used on lakes and moderate rapids.

BUILDING MATERIALS: ALUMINUM

Aluminum canoes are inexpensive, strong, reasonably light, and maintenance free. In the past most of the canoes used by professional outfitters were aluminum, but now crafts built of Royalex and polyethylene are more popular.

Since the machinery that produces aluminum canoes is very expensive, there have been few design innovations. Most aluminum canoe designs are decades old—some date back to the 1940s. Few are very good. Invariably, 18-footers—which are designed for a more knowledgeable market—are best for wilderness travel. Look for hard-tempered aluminum and closely spaced flush rivets. Spot-welded members should be above the waterline.

The greatest drawback of aluminum is its tendency to cling to subsurface rocks—a characteristic that can be minimized by applying paste wax to the hull. Aluminum also dents; and try as you may, you will never remove the dents completely. Old aluminum canoes gradually take on the appearance of a high school shop ballpeen hammer project as they acquire dent upon dent!

FIBERGLASS CANOES

Note: All the best fiberglass canoes are selectively reinforced with Kevlar 49. See the section on KEVLAR for a description of this popular fabric. Now here's a building material that you can get excited about! It's very strong, acceptably light, relatively inexpensive...and the easiest of all canoe building materials to repair. No, it's not as durable as heavy, heat-treated aluminum or polyethylene. So what? If you need more strength than that obtainable in a well-built fiberglass canoe, then you're either willfully abusing your craft or you don't know how to paddle! The fact is that good fiberglass canoes are plenty strong enough for use in any type of water. Granted, the strength advantages of Kevlar over fiberglass are real, but not real enough to justify the hundreds of extra dollars that all-Kevlar construction commands. Buy Kevlar to save weight, not to gain strength!

All the best fiberglass canoes are selectively reinforced with Kevlar 49 in their construction—mostly to reinforce delicate canoe stems and areas that are most subject to abrasion (see page 9 for a description of this popular fabric). Today's "fiberglass composite" canoes are light and strong—a far cry from those available a decade ago.

Construction Methods

There are so many ways to build fiberglass composite canoes that it would require a full chapter to outline them all. To understand the most commonly used procedures, you should know some terminology.

Fiberglass "cloth" is composed of twisted strands of fiberglass that are woven at right angles to one another. Cloth yields the highest glass to resin ratio (about 1:1) of all the fiberglass fabrics and therefore has the greatest tensile strength. Most of the best all-fiberglass canoes are built of "all-cloth" laminates.

Fiberglass matt is composed of chopped cross-linked glass fibers that are held together with a dried resin binder. Matt has a glass to resin ratio of about 1:3, which means it's only about one-third as strong as woven cloth. Its main use is as a stiffening agent in canoe bilges and other places where extreme rigidity is desirable. Canoe hulls can also be stiffened with fiberglass cloth (some are), but this is more expensive, both in terms of labor and material costs.

Roving is a much coarser weave than cloth. Its glass to resin ratio is slightly less than that of cloth, but its impact resistance is greater. It is also used to help stiffen a hull.

Gelcoat: is an abrasion-resistant waterproof resin used on the outside of a fiberglass canoe. Color is in the thin layer of gelcoat, which "scratches white" when you hit rocks. To save a few pounds, some canoes are built without gelcoat (called skin-coat construction). However, skin-coat canoes are more subject to damage from abrasion than are those with gelcoat. A tripping canoe should have a gelcoat finish.

Resins

There are polyester, vinylester, and epoxy resins—and dozens of formulations for each.

Polyester resin is the least strong, least expensive, and the standard of the canoe-building industry.

Vinylester resin may be the best compromise between cost and strength. Vinylester has low toxicity and it's relatively easy to work with. Most of the best Kevlar canoes are now being built with this resin.

Epoxy resin is the strongest of all resins. It is also expensive, difficult to work with, and frequently more toxic than polyester or vinylester. Epoxy is used on a regular basis by only a small number of custom canoe builders. Whether it has enough advantages over vinylester to warrant a higher cost is debatable.

How They're Built

Chopper-gun lay-up: A mixture of chopped strands of fiberglass and polyester resin is sprayed into a mold. The resulting canoe is very heavy, not very strong, and cheap. All the worst canoes are built this way. The telltale matrix of chopped fibers is visible on the inner walls of the craft. Chopper-gun canoes are no bargain at any price.

Hand lay-up: Glass cloth, and possibly roving and matt, is laid into a mold by hand, then saturated with resin and squeegeed out. All-cloth canoes are the toughest and most resilient of the breed; they are also the most expensive. You can tell hand lay-up at a glance— you can see the crisp outline of the glass weave in the inside of the hull.

Vacuum bagging: A plastic vacuum bag is placed into the mold and the air is pumped out. This compresses the resin-soaked laminate and evenly distributes the resin, thus giving you the highest glass/Kevlar to resin ratio possible—all of which translates into a very light, very strong canoe. All the competitive racing canoes are built this way.

Foam cores: A canoe bottom that flexes due to water pressure won't maintain its shape and paddling efficiency. For this reason performance-minded canoeists prefer hulls that are as stiff as possible. The lightest, strongest way to stiffen a canoe is to sandwich a layer of closed-cell foam between the Kevlar or fiberglass laminates. Often, foam ribs are added to increase the torsional stiffness of the sidewalls. The entire boat is then vacuum bagged to eliminate as much resin (and weight) as possible.

Vacuum-bagged foam-core hulls are extremely light. Some Kevlar racing models weigh under twenty-five pounds, and tripping boats of forty-five pounds are a reality. On the surface, you can make a very good case for this type of construction. However, the light stiff, hulls preferred by racers often break when they hit rocks. You need some flex in a wilderness canoe, even if it means sacrificing paddling performance. And because there's less fabric (fiberglass or Kevlar) in a foam-core boat than in an all-cloth one, the hull is more easily damaged. Once the foam core is cut through, cosmetic repairs become difficult. Replacing large sections of damaged foam has been described as similar to performing a lobotomy. Canoes with foam cores are ideal for racing, lazy waterways, or folks who can afford to repair or replace them when they become damaged.

Color: Canoe color is a personal thing, although dark colors add weight to the gelcoat. That's because it takes more color agent to get a dark green or red color than a clear (colorless) or white one. Generally, the darker the color, the heavier the finished canoe will be.

As you have probably guessed, my favorite color is white. White canoes "scratch white" and so hide surface damage. White is also the easiest color to match when making cosmetic repairs—something every canoeist has to do at least once a year.

KEVLAR 49

Kevlar is a honey-gold-colored fabric manufactured by the Du Pont Company. It looks much like fiberglass cloth (and it is used in the same way) only its properties and price are much different. Kevlar 49 composites have a tensile strength about 40 percent higher than epoxy-fiberglass and a specific gravity of 1.45 grams per cubic centimeter, versus 2.55 for glass. This means that canoes built of Kevlar are much stronger and lighter than equivalent glass models. Kevlar is widely used as tire cord fiber and as bulletproof material in flak vests—testimony to its incredible strength. Unfortunately, the fabric is very expensive and difficult to work with, so all-Kevlar canoes typically cost $300 to $600 more than identical fiberglass models.

Unlike fiberglass, Kevlar cannot be sanded. It just frizzes up like cotton candy—the canoe looks like it needs a haircut! Bash enough rocks with a Kevlar canoe and you're certain to expose the "hairy" fibers of the cloth. Repairing the mess requires painting on resin (epoxy, polyester, or vinylester) and cutting off the fibers while the resin is "green." The alternative—and the recommended procedure— is to cover the damaged area with a fiberglass patch, which can be sanded.

For this reason it's best to avoid all-Kevlar construction unless you absolutely, positively want the lightest boat possible. A composite lay-up with S-glass (an abrasion-resistant form of fiberglass) as the outer layer will be more durable, easier to patch, nearly as strong, and less expensive than all-Kevlar construction. Many of the best canoe makers are already building canoes like this. Those that aren't might do so if you request it. Right now, American canoeists are enamored with all-Kevlar canoes, much to the detriment of long-term durability...and repairability.

My preference? A vinylester, *all-cloth* Kevlar canoe with an S-glass outer layer in an all-hand or vacuum-bagged lay-up. Color? White, of course.

POLYETHYLENE

When the first polyethylene kayaks appeared more than a decade ago, they received mixed reviews. Granted, they were strong—you could wrap one around a boulder and later retrieve it intact. But the boats were heavy, and state-of-the-art designs simply didn't exist.

Now, that's old hat. Some of the best whitewater kayaks are now rotationally molded from cross-linked polyethylene.

Given the success of polyethylene kayaks, it was only a matter of time before canoe companies got into the act. The first real success was the Coleman canoe—a less-than-daring, buff-bowed design with a network of interior aluminum tubes for stiffening. At the outset Coleman discovered that unsupported polyethylene sheet simply wouldn't hold its shape unless it was given a helping hand through internal struts, ribs, and keel. But the same metal framework that held the plastic in shape also kept it from giving when the boat smashed headlong into a rock. The result was that these canoes performed better on paper than in the maelstrom of a rocky rapid.

The problem is: How do you stiffen a polyethylene canoe without resorting to internal struts and ribs? Old Town Canoe Company may have found an answer. In 1985 they announced a new use of polyethylene. They sandwiched an expanded polyethylene core between two layers of rotationally-molded cross-linked polyethylene. The result was a tough and rigid boat—one whose properties were similar to that of a sandwiched Royalex hull. And because of the stiffness imparted by the foam core, no internal bracing was necessary.

The attractiveness of cored cross-linked polyethylene centers around its strength, resistance to abrasion, stiffness, and relatively low cost. The finished canoe is still rather heavy and the aesthetics of wood or fiberglass simply aren't there. Nevertheless, if you want a good, tough canoe at an attractive price, this might be the route to go.

ABS (ACRYLONITRILE BUTADIENE STYRENE) AND ABS ROYALEX

Ribbed ABS plastic canoes appeared on the market in the 1960s with high hopes. Within two decades they disappeared without a trace. Good! These boats were neither light nor inexpensive and their designs were just short of dreadful. Even their strength was uncertain. In fact, commercial outfitters who tried conventional ABS canoes in the livery trade found that they literally came apart at the seams! Their one redeeming character was good resistance to abrasion. No canoeist I know will mourn their passing.

However, when expanded to foam (Royalex, made by Uniroyal), ABS is an exceptional canoe-building material. Royalex differs from ordinary ABS plastic in that it is laminated and vacuum formed under intense heat and pressure so that its central core contains many tiny air pockets. The resulting product, called *thermoplastic laminate*, is very strong, naturally buoyant, acceptably light, and fairly expensive.

Royalex canoes are nearly impossible to puncture, and they "snick" over subsurface rocks so easily that even a mediocre canoeist has little difficulty making it through a twisting "rock garden." While paddlers of aluminum canoes are still pushing off rocks, Royalex owners are already hundreds of feet downstream. Unfortunately, Royalex is difficult to form into tight curves, which means that fine entry lines and other features that contribute to high performance are hard to obtain.

Although canoes built of other materials are often lighter and faster, none can match the durability of Royalex. For paddling the unforgiving waterways of the Far North—where you can't afford to have a canoe fail—Royalex is the premier material!

CEDAR-STRIP CANOES—THE ONES THAT WIN RACES

Many of the canoes that win long-distance, flatwater races are hand built of cedar or redwood strips, nailed to a form, glued together, and covered with fiberglass cloth and polyester or epoxy resin (the nails are removed prior to glassing). The result is a very beautiful, very light canoe. Since construction is entirely done by hand, the few companies that produce this style canoe command high prices ($1,000 and up). Strip canoes, however, are easily built by anyone with power tools, basic woodworking know-how, and patience. They are very inexpensive to make. Easy-to-follow plans for the construction of several excellent canoe models are available at low cost from the Minnesota Canoe Association, P.O. Box 13567, Dinkytown Station, Minneapolis, MN 55414.

It is interesting to note that the greatest cross-continent canoe safari of the twentieth century was completed in a canoe built of Sitka spruce strips and fiberglass. In April 1971 Verlen Kruger of DeWitt, Michigan, and Clint Waddell of Saint Paul, Minnesota, launched a hand-built 21-foot strip canoe at Montreal's Lachine docks on the Saint Lawrence River. The two men paddled sixty-five-hundred miles across some of the roughest waterways in North America, and terminated their trip at the Bering Sea in Alaska just five months later. Vital canoe statistics were:

Length: 21 feet
Width measured 3 inches off the bottom: 27 inches
Width measured the center thwart: 34 inches
Depth: 18 inches at the bow; 12½ inches rest of length
Weight: 85 pounds

CANOEING AND CAMPING

Seats: Sawyer molded fiberglass, bucket type
Yokes: Form-fitted center yoke for one-man carry and a pad and yoke at each end for two-man carry.
Cover: 8-ounce waterproof nylon snap-on for complete protection from spray.

Experienced paddlers will recognize Kruger's hand-built canoe as a lengthened version of the standard Canadian racer. The Waddell—Kruger expedition to the Bering Sea is one of the most fantastic canoe voyages of our time—perhaps of any time. The fact that this trip was safely completed in a modern canoe of revolutionary design should do much to dispel the myth that canoes have changed little since the time of the Indian birch barks.

WOOD-CANVAS CANOES

Wood-canvas canoes are making a comeback! The world-famous Chestnut canoes are again being fabricated in Canada, and scores of smaller custom builders have taken up the banner. Prices are competitive with state-of-the-art Kevlar canoes.

A good wood-canvas canoe will weigh about the same as an all cloth fiberglass one, will be nearly as strong, and because its bottom flexes, it will slide over rocks easily. There are many canoeists who feel that absolutely nothing paddles as well as a traditional wood-canvas canoe. Certainly few other canoes are as beautiful.

EASE OF REPAIR

If you use your canoe hard in rocky white water, you will ultimately need to repair it. Canoes built of fiberglass and Kevlar are easiest to repair—a properly applied patch is hardly noticeable. Wood-strip canoes mend nicely, as do wood-canvas ones. It's possible to fix a Royalex/ABS or aluminum canoe, but the patch will be a glaring reminder of the rock you hit. From the aesthetic viewpoint, polyethylene hulls cannot be repaired.

Despite what some canoe manufacturers say, no canoe-building material is indestructible. So consider the merits of a less durable canoe that is easily patched over a more durable one that is not.

BUYING A USED CANOE

Now that you are familiar with canoe design and construction, you should have a pretty good idea of what you want in a canoe. The following guidelines will help you get the best deal on a good used canoe:

1. Know the retail value of the canoe before you talk to the owner. Figure on paying up to 80 percent of the current retail price for well-cared-for, top-line aluminum canoes and around 50 percent for lesser-known aluminum, fiberglass, and ABS cheapies. Quality-built fiberglass, Kevlar, and Royalex canoes are commonly 60 to 75 percent of their new retail cost, if they have been well kept.

2. If you are trying to save money, purchase a canoe with a hole in it. Contrary to popular belief, canoes are easily patched (see chapter 8, Canoe Rescue and Repair). Check with commercial outfitters, who often sell damaged canoes cheaply (shoddy equipment is bad for their image). With ingenuity and the proper repair materials, you can often restore a canoe to nearly new condition.

3. Turn used canoes upside down and sight along the keel. Don't buy a canoe with a "hogged" (bent-in) keel. Once a keel is bent, it is almost impossible to straighten it properly.

4. Carefully sight along each gunwale. It is very difficult to straighten heat-treated aluminum gunwales, although a hammer and a piece of two-by-four can be used to improve aesthetics somewhat. Plastic and wood gunwales that are cracked or broken must be completely replaced.

5. On aluminum canoes check for stressed or pulled rivets, which could cause leakage.

6. Check fiberglass canoes for signs of hull delamination. Home-built and factory prefabricated kit models especially should be carefully examined, as the quality of these canoes depends entirely upon the skill of the builder. This doesn't mean that hand-built canoes are bad. On the contrary, many canoe clubs own their own molds, and club members produce superb canoes at a fraction of the cost (and weight) of factory-built models. A well-constructed club-built canoe may be an excellent investment. Occasionally a racing enthusiast will offer a nearly new canoe for sale at little more than the original cost of the building materials, simply because he or she is displeased with the canoe's performance. Canoe clubs and canoe races are good places to frequent if you are looking for a good, inexpensive canoe.

In summary, select a canoe of adequate size and depth. Be certain that the keel line of the canoe is straight and check for damaged fittings. Eliminate from consideration any fiberglass or Kevlar canoe that shows signs of hull delamination and be knowledgeable of the canoe's value before you buy. Lastly, join a canoe club. Club membership will bring you into contact with skilled paddlers and canoe builders and will increase your chance of locating a good used canoe at a reasonable price.

CHAPTER TWO

Low-Cost Ways to Improve the Performance of Your Canoe

If you want to learn the fine points of canoeing, attend a competitive race event. Flatwater, downriver, or white water slalom—it makes no difference. In every case the name of the game is "winning." And the difference between winning or losing is often a matter of only seconds or tenths of seconds. At the highest levels of competition the performance edge is as much due to the right equipment as it is to the capabilities of the paddlers.

Between races check out the boats. But look beyond the basics of brand names and hull design. Examine instead how the canoes are tricked out—how they're "tuned." Study the seating arrangement: height and support of seats, type of sliding mechanism (if any), location of knee pads, toe blocks, thigh straps, and so forth. What about safety accessories like grab loops and flotation? It won't take you long to discover that these customized race machines are a far cry from what you can buy in the stores.

After the race engage in some friendly banter with the competitors. Artfully turn the subject from racing to fast touring and wilderness tripping. Do your new friends own cruising canoes? If so, what modifications have been performed to make them safer and more comfortable to paddle? Listen intently and bring a note pad. You'll discover a wealth of honestly useful ideas.

Here are some tips you might learn from your conversations with the masters. Emphasis is on low-cost modifications that you can perform on your own canoe.

CARRYING YOKE

Canoes are usually carried by one person with the aid of a padded carrying yoke (an extra-cost item). Aluminum yokes are channeled to fit over the existing center thwart (an exception is the excellent Alumacraft yoke, which is supplied as standard equipment in lieu of a center thwart), while wooden yokes replace the thwart completely. Most manufacturers install the center thwart or yoke in a location determined by a formula, which is often subject to some error. For example, the yoke on one of my canoes was misplaced by 4 inches, making the craft so tail-heavy that it was impossible to carry.

The most satisfactory method of balancing a canoe is to try it on your shoulders. I like just enough weight in the tail that the bow will rise very slowly when the canoe is shouldered. I consider a canoe out of balance if more than gentle pressure is required to bring it back to a horizontal position. You can easily change the balance on your canoe by reinstalling the yoke in a new set of mounting holes drilled in the gunwales.

If you are very broadshouldered, you will like the spacing of factory-made yoke pads; but if you're of average build, you will need to move the pads closer together and change their angle somewhat. Most people prefer pads mounted at right angles to the yoke bar, with a distance of 7½ inches between them.

If you do much portaging, you'll want a wooden yoke. The springiness and warmth of wood against your neck makes for more comfort than the inflexibility and coldness of aluminum. Make your yoke from a good hardwood (ash or oak is best) and finish to ¾ by 2½ inches to insure adequate strength. Cut two 8-by-4-inch yoke-pad blocks from ½ inch pine and pile polyurethane foam on each block (use pillow padding available at any discount store). Compress each pad to about 2½ inches and cover with a light-colored Naugahyde to reflect heat. (I found the difference in surface temperature between a black pad and a white pad in strong sunlight to be thirty-five degrees!) Staple Naugahyde into place and finish with

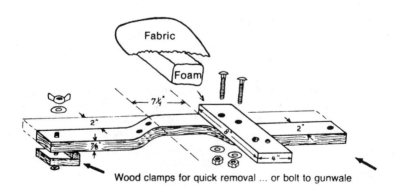

Wood clamps for quick removal ... or bolt to gunwale

Figure 2-1 The yoke should be made with hardwood. The fabric is stretched over the foam and fastened with staples to a 4 x 8-inch wood block. Drainage holes should be drilled through this block.

upholstery tacks. Then drill a few ¼ inch or ⅜ inch-diameter holes through the face of each yoke-pad block so water that accumulates in the foam (when you capsize) will drain out. Commercial yokes don't have drain holes, so moisture becomes trapped in the yoke pads and causes the wood blocks to rot.

Secure your yoke to the gunwales with stainless steel bolts or use the simple clamp device illustrated. Clamp-in, removable yokes are the way to go if you plan to carry a passenger—the yoke can be removed to provide more room for the rider.

SHOCKCORDS AND RUBBER ROPES

On a trip down the flooded Groundhog River in northern Ontario, my partner and I inadvertently ran a 5-foot falls. When the bow of our 18-foot canoe punched through the big roller below, the canoe filled with several inches of water. We spun broadside in the rapids, swamping completely. Fortunately, our four watertight Duluth packs stayed put throughout the run, providing us with sufficient buoyancy to keep afloat. We retained enough freeboard to paddle cautiously ashore.

In white water you need the additional flotation provided by watertight packs, and you can only utilize this flotation if packs are well secured in the canoe. If your canoe is aluminum, drill a series of ⅜ inch-diameter holes along the gunwales about 4-inches apart. These holes will provide anchor points for cords and steel hooks to which heavy-duty rubber ropes are attached. If the gunwales of your canoe have water-drain slots (as on wood-canvas models), you can hook your cords or rubber ropes directly to them. The solid rails of most fiberglass and ABS boats, however, present more of a problem. Usually it is possible to drill small holes through the inwale or just below the gunwale. Short loops of parachute cord can then be run through these holes to provide attachment points for your security ropes.

Run at least two rubber ropes across each pack, and where very heavy-duty rapids will be encountered add a length of nylon parachute cord. Tie the cord with a quick-release knot (see chapter 10, Tying It All Together) so you won't have difficulty salvaging your gear if you overturn. You can stuff your bailing sponge, fishing gear, and loose articles under the ropes to prevent loss in an upset. The parachute cords will prevent *pack-bob* (packs rising up in a water-filled canoe). Rubber ropes permit quick removal and replacement of packs when making portages. It is a real pain in the neck to constantly tie and untie a network of ropes.

Drill holes in thwarts and deck plates and install lightweight, fabric-covered shock cord (figure 2-2 shows the procedure). Wet clothes, maps, and oddities placed under the corded thwarts will stay put in high winds and on portages.

PAINTERS

Painters, or end lines, should be attached as close to the waterline as possible. Where lines are secured to the deck of a canoe, the force of the water acting on the canoe is so distant from the point of attachment of the painters that a quick

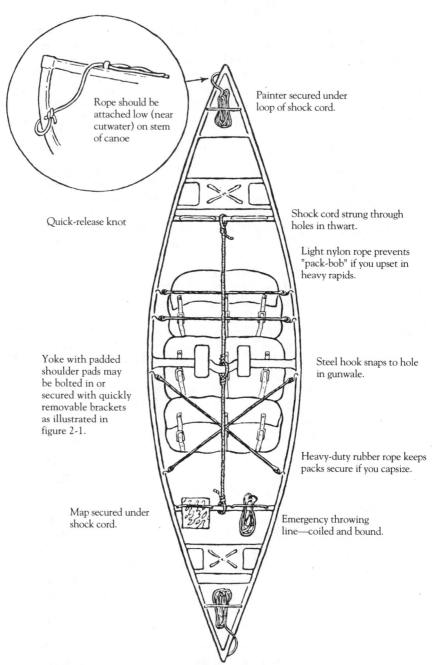

Rope should be attached low (near cutwater) on stem of canoe

Quick-release knot

Painter secured under loop of shock cord.

Shock cord strung through holes in thwart.

Light nylon rope prevents "pack-bob" if you upset in heavy rapids.

Yoke with padded shoulder pads may be bolted in or secured with quickly removable brackets as illustrated in figure 2-1.

Steel hook snaps to hole in gunwale.

Heavy-duty rubber rope keeps packs secure if you capsize.

Map secured under shock cord.

Emergency throwing line—coiled and bound.

Figure 2-2 A "customized" canoe protects your valuables.

pull of a rope can, in some rapids or currents, overturn the canoe. Drill a hole below the deck plate and epoxy in a length of ½ inch diameter PVC water pipe. The tube will keep water from leaking into the canoe when the bow plunges in rapids.

The best way to keep painters available and out of the way is to coil and stuff them under a loop of shockcord attached to the deck. Thus stored, they can be released by a simple tug of the end. They won't stream out independently if you capsize and will remain in place while portaging. Use bright-colored ⅜-inch polypropylene (it floats!) rope for painters.

GRAB LOOPS
Attach a loop of polyethylene rope to each end of the canoe. Should you swamp in rapids, you can quickly grab the loop, which may be more accessible than a painter. Grab loops are also convenient handholds for lifting the canoe.

GLARE REDUCTION
Glare from the deck plate of an aluminum canoe can be hazardous. An easy solution is to paint deck plates flat black.

CANOE POCKETS
Verlen Kruger, who completed a three year cross-continent canoe odyssey of some twenty-eight thousand (!) miles was the probable inventor of "canoe pockets." On an early safari of sixty-five hundred miles (Montreal to the Bering Sea) Verlen installed plastic bicycle baskets in his canoe and used them to store sunglasses, bug dope, and such. The baskets provided no security for valuables in a capsize, but they were handy nonetheless.

A better solution is to sew up an envelope-style bag from waterproof nylon and tie it to a canoe thwart or gunwale. Or buy one of the many "thwart bags" that are commercially available.

CANOE TUMPLINES
A tumpline consists of a wide leather or canvas strap secured to a pack or bundle. The packer places this strap just above his forehead, grabs the tumpline near his head, leans forward into the trace, and takes off down the trail. The early voyageurs routinely carried one hundred and eighty pounds across rugged portages using only this rig. If tumplines have a failing, it is that they exert tremendous pressure on neck muscles, and most modern voyageurs don't have strong enough necks to tolerate this for very long. Consequently, many canoeists use a combination of tumpline and shoulder straps on their packs. By distributing the weight between tumpline and straps, you can carry very heavy loads for short distances in relative comfort.

For years canoeists have been trying to install tumplines on their canoes to make carrying easier. Unfortunately, conventional tumplines are too rigid. When the canoe bounces up, the tump comes off your head and wraps around your neck.

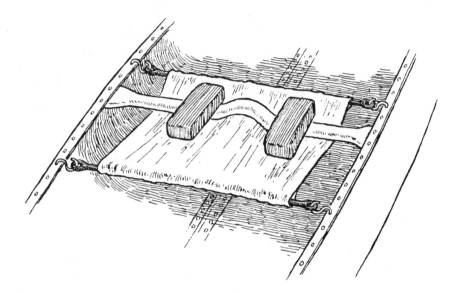

Figure 2-3 A canoe tumpline that works!

Figure 2-4 Ken Saelens models his ingeniously designed tumpline.

CANOEING AND CAMPING

And when the canoe comes down, your head receives the full impact of the weight. Two decades ago I began to experiment with canoe tumplines. At the time I was anticipating an Arctic canoe trip with a thirteen-mile portage. Although I was excited about the trip, I began to have nightmares about carrying my seventy-five-pound canoe across that portage. I figured that with a tumpline, somehow I could make it. I tried rigging one using shock cords, but that didn't work—the thing kept slipping off my head. So I posed the problem to an inventive friend of mine, Ken Saelens. Ken thought a while, then attached a 24-inch length of canvas beneath the yoke of the canoe with two heavy-duty rubber ropes (figure 2-4). The result was dramatic. The tumpline took about 50 percent of the weight off my shoulders, while the canvas eliminated the dangerous possibility of it coming loose and possibly strangling me. In addition, the canvas was handy as a lunch tray and storage shelf for small items.

FOOTBRACES AND/OR KNEE PADS

If you're familiar with the recent canoeing literature, you know that the modern way to paddle a canoe is to sit, not kneel, in it. Right? Not necessarily! Whether you sit or kneel—or alternate between the two—depends on the design of the canoe you're paddling and how you prefer to paddle.

If you have a high-volume Grumman or Old Town Tripper with its high-mounted seats, you'll *have* to kneel in rapids. Purely a matter of getting the CG

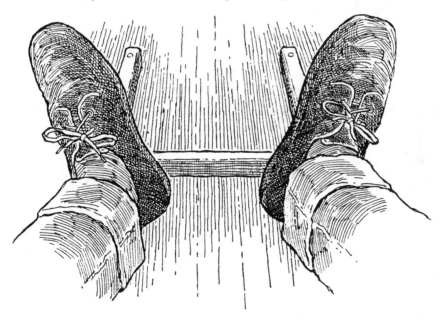

Figure 2-5 Footbraces "lock" you firmly into the canoe when you paddle from a sitting position. The simplest brace consists of a pair of wood rails glassed to the floor of the canoe. An aluminum tube, fastened at the ends, is screwed to the rails.

(center of gravity) low enough for stability in the rough stuff. However, kneeling is practical only if the canoe you're piloting is wide enough at the bow to permit a comfortable kneeling stance (knees spread wide against the bilges). If it isn't—and most fine-lined cruisers are not—then you're best off to maintain your position on the low mounted seat[1] and brace your feet firmly against a bow flotation tank or improvised brace.

If footbraces are important in the bow of a skinny cruiser, they're even more important in the stern. The simplest brace consists of a pair of wood rails glassed to the floor or sidewalls of the boat. An aluminum tube, flattened at the ends, is screwed to the rails.

On the other hand, if your canoe is spacious enough up front for comfortable kneeling, you'll want to raise the seats to a comfortable 10- to 12-inch height (if they're not already set there) and install knee pads. You can purchase self-sticking neoprene pads or make you own from a closed-cell foam trail mattress. Glue knee pads into the hull with contact cement.

Most big tripping canoes provide for both sitting and kneeling options. You may want to install knee pads and footbraces in these boats.

SEAT HEIGHT AND PLACEMENT

I have yet to own a canoe whose seats were placed where I wanted them. Seats on fine-lined cruisers are generally mounted low for stability rather than high for efficiency and all-day comfort.

Many of the best canoes now come with sliding seats, that solves the trim problem when paddlers of different weights are aboard. But seat height is another matter. Most canoeists simply refuse to raise or lower their seats to a height that suits them, falsely believing that it's wrong to tamper with what was obviously ordained by God.

If you don't like the location of your canoe seats, change them, even if it means drilling new holes through the sidewalls of an expensive canoe!

CANOE COVER

Canoe covers are usually home-built affairs. They're constructed of waterproof nylon and have holes (skirts) for the paddlers. They attach to the canoe by snaps, Velcro, or stainless-steel cable.

Some folks swear by canoe covers (I'm one of them). Others swear at them! There's no denying that they cut wind (as much as 50 percent!), keep out rain and white water, and extend the versatility of low-volume canoes—you can use a small canoe in rough water if it is covered. However, covers can be extremely dangerous, especially if they come off in a capsize and entrap you, or if the sprayskirt does not permit an easy exit.

---

[1]Modern fast-cruising canoes generally have seats set 7 to 9 inches off the floor. Seats in tripping and white water canoes are set much higher—10 to 13 inches. The higher the seat, the more comfortable—and tippy—the canoe.

The best setup I've used is a three-piece model of my own design. It has a "belly" section that expands or shrinks as the load height changes. The end caps can be rolled and tied—and may remain on the canoe—while portaging. For solo canoeing I prefer a two-piece cover that I also engineered. Step-by-step instructions for both these designs can be found in my book *Canoeing Wild Rivers*.

Figure 2-6 A three piece canoe cover designed by the author. This model features a "belly" section that expands as the load height changes, and end caps that can be "reefed" while portaging.

CHAPTER THREE

The Necessities

PACKS AND SUBSTITUTES

Frameless Packs

For short, close-to-home trips just about any type of soft pack or duffel bag will do. But for trips of a more serious nature you'll want to invest in authentic packsacks. The most popular and practical for canoeing is the venerable "Duluth pack," which is traditionally constructed of 15- to 20-ounce-per-square-yard canvas. Straps are usually heavy leather and are secured with solid brass rivets and waxed thread. A stout tumpline (head strap) is sometimes provided. Duluth packs are extremely rugged and are commonly sized as follows:

> Number 2: 24 inches wide by 28 inches deep.
> Number 3: 24 inches wide by 30 inches deep.
> Number 4: 28 inches wide by 30 inches deep, with a 6-inch side wall (set out).

The most popular size is number 3, though some canoeists prefer the larger number 4 for lightweight, bulky items like sleeping bags and clothes.

Despite the advent of more modern packs, Duluth packs remain popular. Here's why:

They have a huge capacity—there's always room to stuff one more thing in a Duluth pack.

It's easy to waterproof the contents of these packs by inserting a nested pair of 6-mil plastic bags into them (see "Waterproofing Your Outfit" at the end of this chapter for the specific procedures).

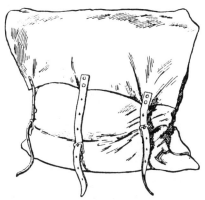

Figure 3-1 The Duluth Pack—still the best choice for canoe tripping.

Duluth packs are designed to sit upright in a canoe instead of on their backs or bellies like packs of more conventional design. This stand-up feature has value when the canoe takes water in rapids or waves. The craft can fill with water and, as long as it remains upright, no water can enter the mouth of the pack. This is because the weakest part of any waterproof bag is its closure, which is just beneath the flap of the erect Duluth pack—out of contact with accumulated water.

Duluth packs fit easily into the unique contours of a canoe without wasting space.

Despite their ominous reputation as instruments of torture, Duluth packs carry easily *if you use a tumpline.* With the headstrap in place (it should rest just above your forehead), the load rides snug against your back. The tumpline should be adjusted so that nearly all of the pack weight is carried on your neck muscles. When you tire of the tumpstrap, simply brush it aside and transfer the weight to the shoulder straps. Once you become accustomed to a tumpline (it takes only a few portages), you'll want one on all your tripping packs. (Traditional canvas Duluth packs are available from Duluth Tent and Awning Company, Box 6024, Duluth, MN 55806, and CLG Enterprises, Box 6687 VSA, Minneapolis, MN 55406.)

State-Of-The-Art Soft Packs

In recent years a number of state-of-the-art canoe packs based on the "Duluth" principal have emerged. Most notable are those made by Grade VI, P.O. Box 8, Urbana, IL 61801, and Granite Gear, 15 Waterfront Drive, Two Harbors, MN 55616.

Both packs utilize straight-through construction (no compartments) and a sophisticated shoulder-harness/hip-belt system that is more comfortable than the standard Duluth. Unlike conventional hiking packs, these units are compact enough to be set upright in a canoe. Either of these packs can double as full-fledged hiking packs. For the past four years I've been using a Grade VI pack, and it earns high marks. Naturally, I added a tumpline!

Packs With Frames

Packs with exterior aluminum frames are an abomination in a canoe. The frames catch on seats, gunwales, and thwarts during loading and unloading operations; the rigid design prevents efficient utilization of space; and they bend or break. I don't know any serious canoeists who prefer frame packs.

Rigid Packs and Wanigan Boxes

Yes, you can carry eggs and Thermos bottles on a canoe trip without breaking them. All you need is a rigid pack of some sort. For centuries the traditional solution has been the woven ash pack basket, which is available from L. L. Bean, Inc., Freeport, ME 04033, and Duluth Tent and Awning Company. I nest my pack basket inside a heavy rubberized army clothes bag and set this combo inside a number 2 Duluth Tent and Awning Company "cruiser" pack. A loop of shock cord seals the mouth of the rubberized bag. This is a very sturdy waterproof unit, and it packs well in a canoe. Order an 18-inch high basket and ask Duluth Tent and Awning Company to extend the closing flap on the

Figure 3-2 The Maine Pack Basket: Items which are breakable or that might be uncomfortable in a conventional "soft" pack are placed in the pack basket. To make a watertight unit, the basket is first placed in a waterproof army clothes bag.

CANOEING AND CAMPING

"cruiser" pack by 8 inches so it will close nicely over the wide mouth of the pack basket.

I'm also very fond of the E. M. Wanigan (E. M. Wanigan, 10411 Kelman Court North, Stillwater, MN 55082), a tough polyethylene plastic box that's portable and watertight…and sized to fit crossways in the belly of the skinniest tandem canoe. The "E. M." has padded shoulder straps and fast, foolproof latches. It holds 5,200 cubic inches of gear—about the same as a number 3 Duluth pack. You can buy the optional hip belt or attach your own tumpline. The box is strong enough to sit or stand on.

Figure 3-3 The E. M. Wanigan: A tough polyethylene box that's portable and watertight. The Wanigan has padded shoulder straps and a 5,200 cubic-inch capacity (about the same as a number 3 Duluth pack).

The portage pannier—a molded fiberglass box that is sized to fit inside a number 3 Duluth pack—is another option. The Portage pannier is available from Wilderness Expedition Products Company, 2516 4th Avenue North, Anoka, MN 55303. The removable lid doubles as a dishpan and cutting board. The unit is reasonably waterproof and strong enough to sit on.

Here are two do-it-yourself alternatives to commercial hard packs: (1) Varnish a large cardboard box inside and out and place it inside your soft pack. For greater longevity, apply fiberglass instead of varnish. (2) Next time you go discount-store shopping, take your Duluth pack with you. When you pass the housewares section, locate a plastic trash can liner that fits inside the pack. The cheaper cans tend to be more flimsy and so conform better to your bony contours than do more expensive rigid models.

Tip: To waterproof the mouth of the plastic trash can, insert the trash can inside a tough plastic bag. This will prevent sharp objects inside the pack from puncturing the delicate waterproof liner. Then, insert the whole combo into your Duluth pack.

WATERPROOF CAMERA BAGS

The best waterproof camera bag I've found is a military-surplus amphibious-assault gas-mask bag. This heavyweight, canvas-covered rubber bag is watertight, rugged, and just the right size to accept a 35-mm camera and telephoto lens. Three solid brass fasteners (they're quiet!) control the opening. To portage, strap the bag on your hip or sling it over your shoulder. Gas-mask bags are available by mail from Thrifty Outfitters, Midwest Mountaineering, Inc., 309 Cedar Avenue South, Minneapolis, MN 55454, or Ruvel & Company, 3037 N. Clark Street, Chicago, IL 60657, "Thrifty" is also your best source for equipment repair. They'll rebuild trail stoves, fix rips in tents and clothing, and refit zippers. They're an authorized repair center for Gore-Tex garments.

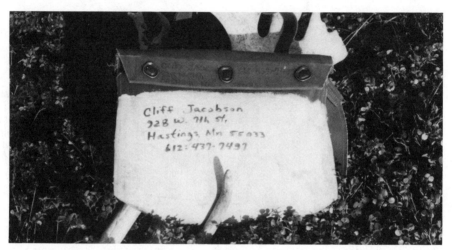

Figure 3-4 The Amphibious-Assault Gas-Mask Bag—the best protection for your camera. It's absolutely waterproof!

TENTS

You can be a bit lavish when selecting a canoe tent. After all, the longest portage in most canoe country is seldom more than a mile—hardly a backbreaking distance to transport a tent of reasonable weight. What's reasonable depends, of course, on your perspective, though most canoeists would agree that twelve pounds is about maximum for a tent that will be used by two people.

Size: It works out that each camper needs a space of around 7 feet by 2 ½ feet just to stretch out and store gear. Increase the area to 8 feet by 3 feet and you enter the realm of "comfort." Widen it another 6 inches and ahhh...pure luxury. A floor plan of 7 feet by 8 feet and enough room to sit fully upright is ideal for two. Evidently most canoeists agree, for nearly all the tents you see on canoe trails are technically classified as "four-person" models even though they're commonly (and wisely) occupied by just two.

Sleeping two in a tent built for four may seem like needless pampering, until:

1. You encounter a storm. Then extra space is essential, not just for sanity but to keep your bedding dry. Even the best tents will deform some in high winds, and if you're snuggled against a sidewall, water is sure to condense on your sleeping bag. And if your tent has a "cap" fly (a three-quarter-length fly that doesn't extend to the ground), wind-driven mist might blow in through the breathable nylon canopy. Now if you can just put some distance between the tent sidewall and your sleeping gear....

2. You become wind- or bug-bound and have to eat, relax, and make repairs to equipment inside your tent.

3. Your neighbor's tent destructs in a high wind or is inadvertently left sitting on a rock at your last campsite. Thank God you have a four-person tent and can handle the overload!

Fabrics: The only suitable tent material is nylon. Cotton tents are too heavy, they gain weight when wet, and they mildew. When you buy a nylon tent, make sure you specify two-ply construction. This means that the tent consists of two layers of fabric. The main tent body is built of a porous nylon or mosquito net, to let body-produced water vapor out. To keep the rain from getting in, a chemically coated waterproof fly is suspended a few inches over the inner tent. The result is a shelter that is completely watertight, breathable, and lightweight. You can pitch the tent without the fly on clear nights, or you can remove the rainfly and use it separately as your only shelter for camping in the fall when bugs are no problem (Some of the best canoe tents have integral flies that cannot be removed).

Bulk: Bulk is more important than weight. You can live with a few extra pounds, even on a go-light canoe journey, but not with a tent that won't fit in your pack. The culprit is usually the length of the poles—sections longer than 23 inches simply won't fit crossways in most packs without protruding from under the closing flap. And anything that's secured by friction alone can work free and be lost.

A good canoe tent should pack small enough to fit completely inside the waterproof confines of your packsack. Unfortunately, some otherwise outstanding canoe tents do not.

Here's how to pack a tent with obnoxiously long poles: (1) Stuff or roll the tent without the poles or pegs. Pack the tent inside your pack. (2) Place poles and pegs in a sturdy nylon bag with drawstring closure. Sew a loop of nylon webbing to each end of the bag and attach lengths of parachute cord to the loops. (3) Pack the pole set under the pack flap and snake the closing straps through loops in the cord ends. Now your pole bag can't possibly fall out of your pack.

Geometry: You'll pay much more for sophisticated geometrics (dome and tunnels) than for simple-to-sew but reliable A-frame designs. Canoe camps are commonly pitched on solid rock, sand, or the pebbles of a passing gravel bar, so choose a tent that is freestanding or nearly so. And be aware that price does not necessarily indicate foul-weather performance or how easy (or difficult) the tent is to pitch.

SLEEPING BAG

Average canoe-country temperatures seldom go below freezing, and in this climate a sleeping bag filled with 20 ounces of good down or 2 pounds of quality synthetic is quite adequate. In fact, I would rule out as too warm any closely fitting bag with more filler than this.

A real advantage of Quallofil™ and Polarguard™ is that these synthetic materials, unlike down, stubbornly refuse to absorb water. If a Quallofil or Polarguard bag gets wet, it can be wrung out and will retain a good share of its warmth. Down, on the other hand, possesses almost no insulating value when water-soaked.

However, as I've already pointed out, there's no excuse for getting your sleeping bag—or anything else—wet on a canoe trip. If you don't know how to waterproof your gear or stormproof your tent, you need to learn the basic waterproofing skills outlined at the end of this chapter.

TRAIL MATTRESS

A good trail mattress should smooth out the lumps and insulate your body from the cold, damp ground. It should also be lightweight, compact, and reliable.

Air mattresses work fine in July heat but become downright cold when temperatures drop below 50 degrees Fahrenheit. When it is cold, you'll want an open- or closed-cell foam pad or a ThermaRest™, a self-inflating foam-filled air mattress that combines the comfort of air with the insulation of polyurethane foam.

For the ultimate in insulation and comfort, team a nylon air mattress with a thin, closed-cell foam pad. This outfit weighs about three pounds, but is very compact.

It's important to realize that any air-filled mattress will eventually fail, so if cost or reliability is a concern, you may want to consider a pure foam product. Whatever you buy, cover it with a breathable cotton shell. Nylon covers are hot and sticky against the skin and they slide out from under your sleeping bag and wander all over the tent floor.

COOKING GEAR

See chapter 15, page 151, for a discussion of essential cooking gear.

STOVES

There are gasoline, kerosene, multifuel (burns any liquid fuel), propane, butane, and wood-burning stoves. For canoeing, gasoline stoves make the most sense. Propane stoves are too heavy, butane models don't put out enough heat, and kerosene stoves are smelly and must be primed. Multifuel stoves are ported to burn a variety of liquid fuels, so they are much less efficient than gasoline models. Gasoline stoves run more efficiently on naptha (Coleman and Blazo brand fuels) than on white gasoline. *Warning:* Do not use unleaded automotive fuel in a stove that is designed to burn white gasoline. Impurities in automotive unleaded gas may create a dangerous condition or cause some stoves to malfunction.

A low-profile gasoline stove with a pressure pump that puts out around 8,500 Btu/hr is best. Store gas in one-liter aluminum bottles or the original metal can. I allow two liters of gas for a party of four people (not including the original stove-tank filling).

One wood-burning stove, the Super Sierra, shows promise. This compact stainless-steel unit is powered by a small fan that runs on a single A-cell battery. The stove has a mechanical damper and weighs just one pound. Heat output at peak efficiency is a remarkable 15,000 Btu/hr. A windscreen, grill, and pot set are available. For details write ZZ Corp., 10806 Kaylor Street, Los Alamitos, CA 90720.

Stove Tricks

- Empty the fuel from your stove after each outing and burn the tank dry at the end of the camping season. Residues from fuel left in stoves is the major reason for stove failure.
- Mix a capful (no more) of carburetor cleaner with half a tank of gas and burn this mixture in your stove at the end of the season to clean out damaging gums and varnishes.
- Keep leather pump washers lubricated with high grade gun oil. Avoid vegetable oils, which can gum up stove parts.
- Replace the rubber gasket inside the stove filler cap at least once every two years. Gaskets harden with age and leak air—a major cause of stove failure.

CUTLERY

Knives

For day tripping any jackknife will do, but for more adventuresome canoeing you'll want a blade that's long enough to produce kindling, slice sausage, and reach the bottom of the peanut butter jar.

Most of the time I carry my old fixed-blade Gerber shorty (4½ inch blade) in a heavy-duty sheath on my hip. A Swiss army knife or Leatherman tool takes care of repairs.

Tip: Select a thin (no wider than ⅛ inch thick across the spine), straight blade with a reasonably sharp point. "Flat-ground" blades are better for slicing meat and vegetables than are those with hollow ground (concave) edges. And high-grade tool steel takes a keener edge and is much easier to sharpen than stainless.

AXE AND SAW

You need an axe for splitting kindling, driving stubborn tent stakes, setting rivets

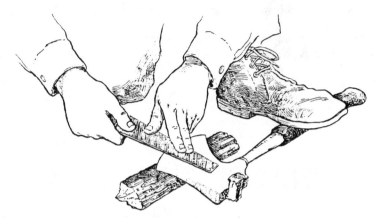

Figure 3-5 Here's the best way to sharpen an axe in the field. When using this method, care must be taken to prevent the file from going too far forward (a bad cut could result). For the utmost in safety, equip your file with a handle and guard (impractical accessories on extended canoe trips).

in torn pack straps, and repairing bent hardware on canoes. But you don't need a big axe. Saw your wood into 12-inch lengths and you'll have no trouble splitting them using the procedure illustrated on page 131.

Most sheaths that come with cutlery are too thin. To make your own sheath, obtain some heavy sole leather and soak it in water for a few minutes until it is flexible. While the leather is wet, mold and cut it to the shape of the tool (you should make a paper pattern first). When the leather is reasonably dry, glue the sheath together with contact cement and seal the edges with brass rivets. Use the procedure illustrated in figure 3-5 to keep your axe keen and free of nicks.

SHOVEL
A foot-long piece of aluminum tubing with one end smashed flat makes an excellent ultralight shovel.

FOOTWEAR
Leather boots get wet and stay that way. For serious canoeing choose from the following:

- Rubber boots with steel shanks and 16-inch high tops. These are preferred mostly by Canadian bush travelers, who often wade icy rivers.
- Rubber-bottom-leather-top shoe-pacs of the L. L. Bean type—popular with canoeists who want more support, comfort, and breathability than provided by all-rubber boots.

- Inexpensive tennis shoes and wool socks. For chilly March white water, wear neoprene wet-suit socks inside oversize sneakers.
- River sandals are great for wading rocky stream bottoms when the water is warm. **Tip:** Buckles and laces hold better than Velcro tabs.
- Reef-runners are flexible nylon moccasins that slip on and secure with a Velcro tab. Designed for surfboarding and sailing, they work well for warm-water canoeing where there are no portages.

For wilderness canoeing you need an extra pair of boots or shoes. I wear 12-inch "Bean" boots for most of my paddling and switch to supple, high-topped canvas sneakers for wading and relaxing.

PERSONAL CLOTHING

For one- or two-day trips bring a complete change of clothes. For outings longer than two days add two changes of underwear and three or four pairs of socks. Be sure to take a medium-weight wool jac-shirt or pile sweater and nylon windbreaker. Canoe-country temperatures seldom go below freezing, so there really is no need to take additional clothing.

Regardless of the clothing you select, it should be unrestrictive to allow freedom for paddling. Shirts and jackets should be comfortable to wear under a life jacket. For this reason bulky down and fiberfill jackets are not recommended. Your canoeing wardrobe should consist almost exclusively of wool, polypropylene, or pile for warmth and quick-drying nylon for wind and water protection. Cotton is acceptable only for wind parkas or for use in very warm weather.

Long Johns

For chilly spring canoe trips, long johns are a must. Polypropylene, pile, Dacron, and wool all work well, and differences between these fabrics are less pronounced than manufacturers will admit. *Warning:* Some fabrics (notably polypropylene and certain Dacron blends) absorb body odors and smell awful in a short time. And insect repellents dissolve some synthetics instantly.

Rain Gear

The best rain gear is a two-piece coated nylon rain suit. Avoid ponchos and below-the-knee rain shirts; these can make swimming difficult if you capsize.

If you want a reliable, inexpensive rain suit, check out the ones at industrial-supply stores—the same places where construction workers shop. The new industrial rain suits are very light and are constructed of fabrics that are similar to those used on the best foul-weather suits. But because there are no pockets, form-fitted hoods, or other niceties, they cost much less.

At the far end of the cost spectrum are PVC and neoprene-coated foul weather sailing suits—they won't let you down no matter how bad it rains. They are worth every penny if you need them and can afford them.

Early Gore-Tex garments often leaked when they became soiled, but the "new generation" stuff is reliable, even when dirty. Be sure to specify rainwear-without-compromise (RWC) construction on all Gore-Tex foul-weather gear. Garments that do not have the RWC tag may leak in prolonged rain.

Buy what you can afford, but don't waste your money on frills you don't need. And get your outfit large enough to fit over baggy trousers and a life vest. Rains are frequently sporadic in canoe country; stripping off a life jacket every time you want to put on or take off your rain gear is a hassle. Incidentally, some rain trousers are equipped with snaps or Velcro at the ankle, which severely restricts ventilation. Rain trousers should hang straight and "pump" air with every move you make.

Finally, be aware that even the best rain gear will develop holes if you wear it all the time. So wear rain clothes only when it rains and switch to a lightweight, breathable nylon shell for protection from wind.

See Appendix 2 for a checklist of essential personal and community gear.

WATERPROOFING YOUR OUTFIT

If money is no object, you can buy state-of-the-art neoprene or PVC-coated packsacks that are guaranteed not to leak—at least when new. And you can patch, glue, and ultimately replace them after a few dozen mean portages. That's because no matter how substantial a pack fabric is, it will ultimately succumb to the effects of abrasion. For example, how long will the best PVC-coated pack last when it's loaded with sixty pounds of gear and dragged solidly across sharp granite or slammed hard onto a pebble beach? These are the harsh realities of wilderness canoe travel.

The inner fabric of a packsack is also subject to considerable abrasion. Every time you stuff a pair of sneakers, hand-axe, or sleeping bag deep inside the pack, you rub off a microthin layer of its waterproof coating. Eventually, the bag will leak and you'll need to repair it. Far better to devise a waterproof system that can be maintained at low cost—one that will keep water out and provide the abrasion protection you need.

The key to the system is to sandwich inexpensive plastic bags between layers of abrasion-resistant material. For example, to waterproof your sleeping bag, first stuff the bag into its nylon sack (which need not be watertight), then set the sack inside a 4-mil-thick plastic bag. Pleat and twist the end of the bag, fold it over, and secure it with a loop of shock-cord. Then, place this unit into an oversize nylon sack (again, it doesn't have to be waterproof). Note that the delicate plastic liner—which is the only real water barrier—is protected from abrasion on both sides!

If you line your nylon stuff sack with a plastic bag, then stuff your sleeping bag into it as advised by some authorities, you'll abrade and eventually tear the plastic liner. The method I've suggested creates a waterproof seal and eliminates the damage caused by the most careful stuffing.

To make a Duluth pack (or any other soft pack) completely watertight, you'll need two 36-inch-by-48-inch, 6-mil-thick plastic bags. Order these tough plastic bags from Indiana Camp Supply, Inc. P.O. Box 2166, Loveland, CO

80539. Don't use anything you can buy at the supermarket. Even the strongest grocery bags are too weak.

Nest two of these 6-mil-thick bags inside each Duluth pack. The inner bag can be well worn—even have some pinholes—as it functions merely as an interior abrasion liner for the absolutely watertight plastic bag outside.

PACKING OUT

For a trip of one week, you and your partner will need three number 3 Duluth packs or two Duluth packs and a 3-peck (18-inch high) pack basket. Canoe partners should pack together as follows:

Duluth pack number 1: Place the two "waterproofed" sleeping bags in the bottom of the Duluth pack. Set your foam pads or air mattresses on top and complete the package with one or two clothes bags. Each canoeist should have his or her own clothes bag. This is a 10-inch-by-20-inch waterproof stuff sack into which all your clothes and personal gear is placed.

When the pack is completely filled with gear, exhaust the air (give it a hug) then pleat and roll the inner abrasion liner down tight. Atop this place your tent or rain tarp. This isolates items that may be damp or wet from the dry contents of the pack below. It also "barricades" the mouth of the reasonably watertight abrasion liner.

Next, twist, fold over, and secure the waterproof plastic outer bag with a loop of shockcord or a band cut from an inner tube.

You now have a completely watertight pack—one that will withstand the abrasion of stuffing and dragging. Note that the sleeping bag—your most important item—has been placed at the bottom of the pack. Here's why: To reach the sleeping bag, water must first penetrate the moth of the outer waterproof sack (unlikely, if you've sealed it properly). That which does get in must bypass the tent or tarp below, then trickle through the folds of the abrasion liner and work down through nearly 2 feet of gear to the "sandwiched" sleeping bag.

As you can see, there's no reason why you should ever get your sleeping bag wet on a canoe trip!

Duluth pack number 2: Place the nylon bags containing your food in this pack. Organize soft items so they won't gouge your back. If you select dehydrated and freeze-dried foods, a two-week supply for two people will take up about half the pack. The remaining space can be filled with sundries. Everything should be placed in nylon stuff sacks—more for utility than protection from the rapids. Items that must be kept dry are "sandwich-bagged" in the same manner as the sleeping bag.

Seal the waterproof liners as explained, place your rain gear on top, and cinch down the closing flap.

The pack basket: Place your cook kit, in its protective stuff sack, in the bottom of the pack basket. Atop this set your stove and gasoline, Thermos, repair and first-aid kits, fishing reel and lures, handaxe, and other items that are breakable or might be uncomfortable in a soft pack. Seal the waterproof liner and cinch down the pack flap.

PACKING THE CANOE

Place the food pack directly behind the yoke, centered in the canoe. This is your heaviest load and you want it perfectly balanced. Set your pack basket on the other side of the yoke and put your light clothes pack next to the pack on the side of the lightest paddler. This should provide sufficient weight to level the canoe. If a fourth pack is carried, as on extended trips, packs can be placed sideways (parallel to the gunwales) in the canoe. The important thing is to have a low, well-balanced load, with the major portion of the weight as close to the middle of the canoe as possible.

Finish loading by installing your shock-corded security system as explained in chapter 2. If you capsize, your gear will be locked tightly in place and the canoe will float high. Figure 2-2 shows the procedure.

OVER THE PORTAGE AND THROUGH THE WOODS

The standard procedure for portaging is as follows: Each person takes a pack and a paddle and strikes out across the portage. While walking, both canoeists look for shortcuts back to the river or lake ahead as well as obstacles that will have to be circuited when the canoe is brought over the trail. Packs are dropped at the end of the portage, and the pair returns. On the second trip one person carries the canoe and the other person takes the last pack and any remaining items. Usually the person with the pack leads so that when the canoe-carrier becomes tired, he or she can call to the person ahead to look for a suitable stopping place—like an out-jutting tree limb where the bow of the canoe can be set. When such a limb is found, the canoe-carrier sets the bow in place and steps from beneath the yoke to rest. This procedure requires much less energy than setting a canoe on the ground and later lifting it to the shoulders.

In heavily traveled wilderness areas wooden rests are often provided to prevent people from jamming canoe ends into tree branches. Although such rests spoil the primitive nature of the portage, they are essential to minimize environmental damage to foliage. In parklike areas where portages are known to be clear and in good condition, the canoe is sometimes carried over the trail first—primarily because it is the heaviest load and requires the greatest expenditure of energy.

PART TWO

Canoe Skills

CHAPTER FOUR

Portaging the Canoe

very canoe trip includes some sort of portage—be it the innocent task of loading the canoe onto the family station wagon, carrying it to and from the launching site, or lifting it over fallen trees, dams, and other obstacles in a local stream. And if you're off to the wilds of Canada, portaging is part of the daily routine.

Although canoes, equipment, and paddling methods have changed considerably during the past century, the technique of portaging has remained the same. I say "technique" because portaging is as much an art as it is a feat of physical strength. I've seen ninety-pound girls singlehandedly lift seventy-pound canoes and carry them nonstop over very rough trails for more than a quarter of a mile. And I've known two-hundred pound men who couldn't carry the same canoe more than 200 feet without profanely dropping it on the nearest boulder. A canoe on land is out of its native habitat, and in the hands of a careless person it may suffer great damage.

The trickiest part of portaging is getting the canoe from the ground to your shoulders. Even old-timers who've sweated under the yoke for more miles than they can recall appreciate a helping hand here. Nonetheless, with a bit of practice, shouldering a seventy-five pound canoe is easy. In fact, once you get the mechanics down pat, you may prefer to loft it yourself rather than trust the outcome to a well-meaning friend who is not familiar with the process.

Surprisingly, it's almost always easier to carry a canoe alone than with a friend, because partners can rarely coordinate their movements. When one person "bounces," the other "jounces"—all of which makes for a terribly awkward and painful experience. Two- person carries are only efficient on groomed trails, and then only when the canoe is outfitted with a yoke at each end.

Except in wind, a healthy adult can usually manage a canoe of reasonable weight (up to eighty-five pounds) without help if he or she has a good yoke and knows the proven lift-and-carry procedures.

ONE-PERSON LIFT AND CARRY

On wilderness trips I seldom pick up a canoe by myself. It just takes too much effort, and I would rather save my energy for the portage trail. However, there will be many times when you will need to lift a canoe to your shoulders alone, so you should become proficient in the one-person lift and carry.

Procedure

If you're right-handed, stand at the center left side of the canoe, facing it. Pull the canoe up by the near gunwale and grasp the center of the yoke with your right hand (figure 4-1). Keeping your legs well apart, flip the canoe onto your thighs with a quick pull of the right arm. As the canoe comes up, grab the far gunwale with your left hand just forward of the yoke (the canoe should now be almost wholly supported by your thighs). Next, transfer your right hand position just back of the yoke on the gunwale (figure 4-2). Thus, your left hand is forward of the yoke on the top gunwale and your right hand is just behind it on the bottom gunwale.

The next part is the hardest. With a quick upward push from your right knee, snap the canoe up and around, over your head (figure 4-3), and settle the yoke pads on your shoulders (figure 4-4). Many beginners have difficulty here because they are fearful of getting their necks twisted up in the yoke. In reality this almost never occurs. It's sort of like closing both eyes and touching your nose with a fist. Just as you always seem to successfully locate your nose, so too will you always find the portage yoke when the canoe comes up.

The key to lifting the canoe is determination and a quick snap. You would have to be very strong to pick up even a light canoe slowly, whereas a person of small stature will have little difficulty raising canoes weighing up to ninety pounds if he or she is snappy about it. When teaching this lift to new canoeists, I often tell them to remember right, left, right to insure that their hands will be properly positioned during the pickup sequence. Thus, the right hand grasps yoke center and the canoe is spun to the thighs; the left hand grasps the top gunwale forward of yoke; right hand grasps lower gunwale just back of yoke and canoe is snapped to shoulders.

The key to carrying a canoe is not strength at all; rather, it is learning to relax under the portage yoke. In order to accomplish this successfully, it is best that you have one or two friends help you position the canoe on your shoulders. When the yoke pads settle into place, stand perfectly straight and reach forward with your hands to grasp the gunwales. Place your fingers on the shelflike lip of the gunwales and your thumbs on the opposite side. If the canoe is properly balanced (slightly tail-heavy), light pressure from your fingers will bring the bow down to a horizontal position. The canoe is now ready for portaging. To get used to the yoke, stand in place and drop your left arm to your side. Most of the canoe's

Figure 4-1 One-Person Lift, Step 1: Right hand grasps yoke center and canoe is spun to thighs.

Figure 4-2 Step 2: Left hand grasps top gunwales forward of the yoke and canoe is balanced on thighs. Note location of right hand.

Figure 4-3 Step 3: With a quick upward push from your right knee, snap the canoe up and around, over your head.

Figure 4-4 Step 4: Settle yoke pads on your shoulders and . . . relax!

CANOEING AND CAMPING

weight will now rest on your right shoulder. Repeat, dropping the other arm. You will become less tired on portages if you continually change the weight from shoulder to shoulder.

TWO- OR THREE-PERSON LIFT, ONE-PERSON CARRY

The two-person lift is identical to the one-person lift except that your helper stands next to you, behind the yoke, and you stand slightly in front of it. The canoe should be supported on the thighs of both you and your partner prior to raising it into position. Your hands will be forward of the yoke and your partner's will be behind it. At a mutually agreed upon signal, flip the canoe, with the help of your partner, up onto your shoulders.

For a completely effortless pickup, try the three-person lift. This is identical to the two-person lift except that you have an additional person. Position yourself at the yoke and have one helper stand at the bow thwart and another helper at the stern thwart. Again, you should all be on the same side of the canoe. All lift together. Nothing could be simpler.

END LIFT

The end lift is an easy way for one or two people to get a heavy canoe up. Stand at the right rear of the canoe, facing the stern. Reach across with your right hand and grasp the left gunwale near the stern seat. Grab the right gunwale with your left hand (figure 4-5). Now just roll the canoe over on its front end (figure 4-6) and lift the tail in the air (figure 4-7). While holding the canoe high, bow on the ground, shuffle yourself forward into the yoke. If you have a helper, let him or her hold the canoe up while you snuggle into the yoke.

The end pickup is popular with persons who for one reason or another don't feel confident using the standard side lift. Although lifting a canoe by one end is accepted practice, it is not good canoeing technique, mainly because the end in contact with the ground gets chewed up.

RACING CARRY

Each paddler places his or her end of the canoe (usually right side up) on a shoulder and cradles an arm around it for support. Once the canoe is in position, racers take off at a run and make very good time over short distances.

WHERE'S THE PORTAGE

Much of North America's canoe country consists of a maze of lakes connected by waterfalls, rapids, and meandering streams. In some cases you can run the rapids or walk the streams. Often, you will have no recourse but to pack your canoe and gear over rugged portage trails.

In frequently traveled areas a portage may be marked by a sign, blazed tree, jutting pole, or small opening in the forest. On isolated routes there may be nothing to mark the way, yet a route around impassable water often exists. Most portages are trampled into place by large animals like moose and bear, who, like you, need to get around rapids and falls. It remains for you to find these trails.

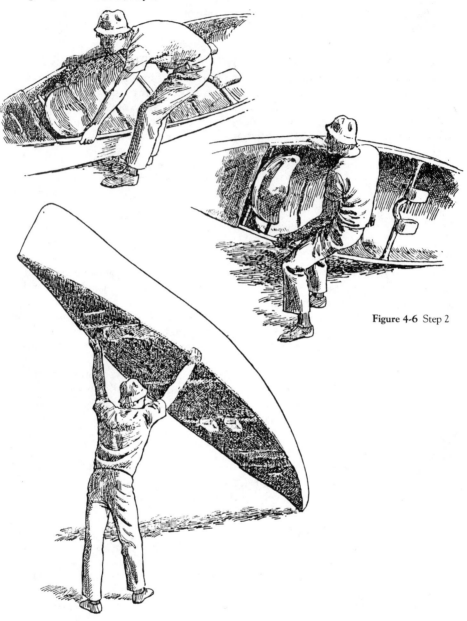

Figure 4-5 The End Lift, Step 1.

Figure 4-6 Step 2

Figure 4-7 Step 3

CANOEING AND CAMPING

Portages are most often located on the inside curves of rivers, and this is where you should look first. When you hear the roar of rapids and see the white plumes of dancing horse tails leaping high into the air, immediately get to the inside bend and paddle ashore. Then, get out of your canoe and start looking. Walk the rapids to see if they are safe to run. Sometimes a single hidden ledge can make a rapid unnavigable, and you may not be able to see the ledge until it is too late!

The absence of a portage does not mean that the rapid is safe to run. Unusually high water may flood existing portages, making them impossible to find, and very low water can change channel characteristics so completely that you may paddle right by the portage without seeing it.

In some areas, especially those near James and Hudson bays, portages are so overgrown with vegetation that you may have to hack your way through a maze of brush to reach safer water at the end of the trail. Cutting paths through the bush is not in keeping with the modern wilderness ethic (leave only footprints, take only pictures), but occasionally, for reasons of safety, you may have no other choice. Fortunately for the environment, the scrubby trees you destroy will quickly grow back.

Never underestimate the power of rapids, especially if the water is high. The rule of thumb in the wilderness is: If in doubt, portage! Develop your whitewater skills at home, not on an isolated canoe trip where a single error can be fatal.

CHAPTER FIVE

Paddle Power

Although paddling a canoe today is much the same as it was a century ago, better equipment and techniques have made it possible for canoeists of limited experience to successfully negotiate rapids that two decades ago were considered impossible. Modern canoesits use paddle strokes that are more powerful, efficient, and less demanding of energy than those used by less scientific paddlers of the past. As a result, a whole new style of canoeing has evolved—a style geared to the superbly designed responsive canoes and ultralight equipment of today.

Some of our best competitors in both whitewater and flatwater events have been paddling for only a few years, yet they would put a professional North Woods guide to shame. While experience is still the best teacher, you can gain a great deal from watching others and reading good books. It may surprise you to know that whitewater canoeists often learn their basic skills in swimming pools. In fact, some very good scores in slalom competition have been posted by first year paddlers who never saw a river before their first event.

This is not to say that experience on wilderness waterways is not valuable. But you can learn to handle your canoe efficiently on the calm lakes and rivers near your home. First, however, you will have to forget much of what you learned from traditional books of the past.

EQUIPMENT FIRST—THE CANOE PADDLE

You can't play good hockey without skates that fit right, and you can't make a canoe respond to your whims without a well-balanced, efficient paddle. Good paddles are expensive, but this is one place you should not try to save money. A fine paddle will bring pleasure with every use. A poorly built paddle will be heavy, ugly, and awkward to use.

First Consideration: The Right Length

Nearly every text on canoeing offers these time-worn formulas for selecting the proper length paddle: (1.) Nose to toes: The grip should reach your nose when the paddle is stood upright. (2.) Chest span: Stretch out your arms; the length of the span equals the length of the paddle. (3.) A bowman should use a paddle that comes to his nose; a sternman should select one that comes to his eyes or the top of his head.

Nonsense! Any recipe for length must take into account the kind of canoe you're paddling, the height of the seats, the length of your torso, the reach of your arms, your own strength, and how you "prefer" to paddle (dynamic racing/switch style or slow-paced, NorthWoods J-stroke. See the paddling section that follows).

As you can see, picking the correct paddle length depends on a number of variables, all of which are interrelated. For this reason experienced canoeists often own a shedful of paddles, each designed for a specific purpose and paddling style.

Let's dissect the variables that affect paddle length:

Seat Height. Seats on the typical high-volume aluminum or Royalex canoe are set relatively high (11 to 13 inches off the floor) for comfort, while those on the modern fine-lined cruiser are slung low (7 to 9 inches) for stability. The higher you sit, the longer the paddle and vice versa. What works best in one style canoe may be terribly awkward in another.

Length of arms and torso, and strength. The length of your torso and reach of your arms also affects paddle length. Long-armed persons who sit tall in the saddle can comfortably wield long paddles; short persons with short arms should do the opposite. Strength is an important factor, too—a strong person can naturally handle a long lever arm (long paddle) more easily than a weak person. Table 5-1 will give you a good starting point for length without resorting to scientific measurements.

Table 5-1 Suggested Straight Paddle Lengths for Use in the Following Canoes*

	Tandem Canoes		Solo Canoes	
Persons with . . .	Stock aluminum and Royalex canoes (Grumman, Old Town Tripper, Mad River Explorer, etc.)	High performance cruisers (Sawyer Cruiser, We-no-nah Jensen's, etc.)	Racers and fast cruisers (Sawyer Summersong, We-no-nah Advantage, etc.	Freestyle and white water canoes (Mad River Ladyslipper, Galt Dandy, Blue Hole Sunburst, etc.)
Short torsos/ short arms	54 inches	52 inches	52 inches	56 inches
Average length torso and arms	56 inches	54 inches	54 inches	58 inches
Long torsos/ long arms	58 inches	55 inches	55 inches	62 inches

* NOTE: These are "guidelines." They *are not* engraved in stone! Bent-shaft paddles (see discussion on page 49) should be about two inches shorter.

Here's the procedure if you want to get technical: (1.) Set your canoe in the water and climb aboard. (2.) Measure the distance from your nose (height of the grip) to the water. That's the *shaft* length. To this add the length of the blade (20 to 25 inches, depending on paddle style). That's the correct paddle length for you. Note that the overall length of the paddle is in part programmed by the blade length.

If you want to get more scientific, you can add in another variable—the weight of your tripping outfit. The more gear you pile into the hull, the lower it will sit in the water, and the shorter your paddle must be.

Nonetheless, unless you're a masochist with figures, your original estimate—or the suggested length I've listed—will get you around in fine style.

To size a paddle without a canoe, stack up some books to equal the height of your canoe seat. Now, sit down and measure from the floor to your chin. This would be the correct shaft length if your canoe rode on top of the water. Now decrease the measured shaft length by an amount equal to the expected draft of your canoe.

Straight-shaft flatwater slalom and whitewater paddles may be 2 to 4 inches longer than the formula measurement.

Paddle length is also a function of how you choose to paddle. Couple a fast cadence with a side switch (HUT!) every six strokes, and you'll want a short paddle. For carving effective turns, you'll want the extra reach of a long paddle.

Gripping the paddle: Most people hog down on the shaft when they should be choking up. There should be 2 to 3 hands distance (roughly equal to the freeboard of your canoe) between your lower hand and the paddle throat. Choking up reduces leverage, but it significantly increases reach.

Straight or Bent Paddle?

As its name implies, bent paddles have their blades offset at an angle. Bends of 5 to 17 degrees are available, although 14 degrees is the most popular.

The bent shaft is more efficient because when you complete a forward stroke with a straight paddle, the blade is in a "climbing" position upon recovery—it *lifts* water and consequently slows the canoe. But the forward bend of the angle paddle puts the blade perpendicular to the water at the end of the stroke, so no water is lifted and no speed is lost. All energy is transmitted into forward motion.

Bent paddles are more efficient than straight paddles, and that's why every canoe racer and performance-minded cruiser uses them. However, they are not ideal for all types of canoeing. They're a bit awkward in rapids and they don't lend themselves to the powerful steering strokes of North Woods style (J-stroke) paddling.

Should you buy a bent-shaft paddle? Absolutely! Granted, bentblades perform best in skinny canoes in which you don't have to reach far over the side to paddle. But they offer enough advantage in wide-bowed aluminum and Royalex canoes to warrant serious consideration. Every canoeist needs at least two paddles, and no rule says they must both be the same. My advice? Get a straight blade for whitewater and a bent-shaft for cruising.

Size your bent paddle about 2 inches shorter than your favorite straight shaft. For the utmost power select a 14- to 15-degree bend; for the greatest control opt for a 10-degree bend. Some manufacturers offer paddles with 5-degree bends, but these offer no advantages over models with straight shafts.

Blade Style

There are dozens of blade styles, but all are variations of the basic shapes outlined in figure 5-2. Some canoeing texts suggest that blade shape is unimportant, but that's not quite correct. Paddles, like canoes, are designed for specific purposes, and each blade style has its place. The four shapes outlined in figure 5-2 pretty much cover the gamut of canoeing possibilities.

Cruising paddle. The modern laminated cruising paddle has straight sides, a squared-off tip, and fairly abrupt shoulders. The 7½ to 8-inch-wide blade provides plenty of surface area for making time in aerated water, yet the blade is narrow enough for effective control. Long-bladed paddles are best suited to use in deep lakes; short- bladed ones are the choice for shallow rivers.

Racing paddle. The wide tip provides plenty of surface area in shallow rivers (where you can't submerge the whole blade), and the tapered shoulders allow you to bring the blade very close to the canoe for greater power and less frequent directional correction. The short blade also means less weight, thus faster recovery at the end of the stroke.

Beavertail. Most ancient of the blade shapes, the beavertail took its form as the most efficient shape that could be cut from a single 6-inch-wide board. When

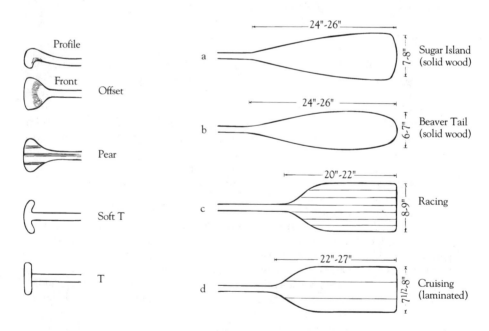

Figure 5-2 Blade styles.

CANOEING AND CAMPING

good waterproof glues were developed, the modern laminated paddle evolved and all but replaced the venerable beavertail.

However, beavertail paddles are making a mild comeback among both traditional North Woods canoeists and those who favor the solo art. The long, narrow, somewhat whippy blade of the beavertail makes subtle steering, alá northwoods style (J-stroke), remarkably easy. A good solid ash beavertail paddle is strong (it has no square corners to break off), beautiful, and much more efficient than most modern canoeists like to admit.

Sugar Island. A modification of the beavertail, the Sugar Island has its greatest width at the tip, which makes it better for use in shallow and aerated water (rapids). The Sugar Island style is favored by some of the best freestyle solo canoeists.

A Summary of Factors that Affect the Choice of Blade Shape:

1. A long, narrow blade is best for steering maneuvers required in North Woods style and freestyle solo canoeing.
2. A wide blade is best for use in shallow and aerated water.
3. The wider the blade, the more awkward and noisy it will be when pulled through the water. Avoid wide blades if wildlife photography and fishing are your main reasons for canoeing.
4. Paddles with splines (vertical ribs) down the center tend to be noisy when pulled through the water, and they are poorly adapted to side-slip maneuvers.
5. Stiff-bladed paddles are best for use in aerated water, while those with reasonably flexible blades are preferable for all-around canoeing.
6. Too much flex in a paddle blade—as evidenced by some inexpensive plastic paddles—is bad. You can't paddle well with a blade that rubberbands through the water!
7. Blades with square corners take a substantial beating in rocky areas. Square tips must be reinforced with a synthetic material (fiberglass, Kevlar, Lexan) to keep them from breaking off in shallows.
8. Square-tip paddles exhibit rotational torque if they're not set into the water exactly perpendicular. For this reason, beginners should avoid them—or round the corners on a wide radius.

Which shape is for you? I suggest you start with something that resembles a cross between paddles A and C—8 inch-wide blade, tapered edges, and rounded tip. This design will perform a multitude of tasks well.

Grip Style

There are Tgrips, pear grips, modified Ts and offset grips. What is best is a matter of preference, although there are some loose guidelines:

1. Tgrips provide precise control of the blade angle—a reason why nearly every serious whitewater canoeist chooses them.

2. There are "good" and "bad" pear grips. The best ones—which are never found on cheap paddles—come very close to complete perfection and are ideal for every use except perhaps the hairiest whitewater.
3. Offset grips are best adapted to the bent paddle, as they put the center of your hand in line with the force of the paddle blade. You'll also find offset grips on some good straight paddles. Whether or not this is a good idea is debatable.

Most canoeists will probably be happiest with a generous pear or "soft" Tgrip. The one place where a Tgrip is out of place is in the modern freestyle canoe. Freestyle technique requires a number of unorthodox moves, many of which require a slightly rotated grip on the paddle.

Weight

The lighter the paddle, the better. Period!

Balance

The best paddles transmit a feeling of "unawareness of the blade" when you heft them.

PADDLE STROKES

The Bow, Or Forward, Stroke

To make the forward stroke most effective, reach as far forward as you can, but don't lunge. Put the paddle into the water at least 2 feet in front of your body. At the start of the stroke the top arm is bent and the lower arm is straight. At the end of the stroke the positions are reversed. Keep your top hand low—below your eyes—and *push*. Most of the power in the stroke should come from pushing with the top hand, not from pulling with the bottom. The stroke is smooth and powerful, and the control is in the top hand. Paddle parallel to the keel, as close to the canoe as possible, and don't bring your lower hand beyond your hip. Bringing the paddle farther back than necessary wastes energy and power, and in

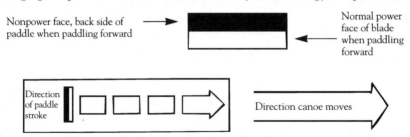

Figure 5-3 Diagrams in this book will use this identification system.

Figure 5-4 Forward Stroke: Put your paddle in the water at least two feet in front of your body. Keep your top hand low below your eyes.

fact actually slows the canoe because the paddle lifts water rather than pushes it straight back.

At the end of the stroke, "feather" (blade face parallel to the keel line) your paddle forward to the starting point so the wind won't catch it and slow you down.

Solo adaptations: When straight-ahead power is applied to one side of a solo canoe, it will veer away from the paddling side. Two or three strokes (perhaps as many as four in a purebred solo racing canoe) is about maximum before the boat turns off course. To correct for this, traditionalists will use the Solo-C, a variation of the J-stroke (described on page 65)—or a highly pitched version of the forward stroke. The alternative is to simply power ahead and switch sides when the need arises—a procedure best adapted to the short bent paddle.

The Back Stroke

Most canoeists pick up the back stroke out of necessity when a large rock looms ahead and they need to avoid it. Other names given to this stroke are "help!", "good grief!", and "@##&**!" It is the exact opposite of the forward stroke, and all comments made about that stroke apply here.

If you're serious about whitewater, you'll want to learn the back draw—an alternate form of the backstroke. The back draw is identical to the draw stroke explained below, except the power is applied parallel to the keel line of the canoe instead of at a right angle to it.

Procedure: Rotate your torso nearly 180 degrees (you're looking straight back towards the stern of the canoe) and "draw." The canoe will move smartly backwards. Though not necessarily more powerful than the conventional back stroke, the back draw allows you to turn your body and look backward in the direction you are paddling. It also permits instant transfer to the draw stroke without sacrificing control—a must when executing the back ferry, which is explained in chapter 6.

Solo adaptations: Here again the problem is keeping the solo canoe on course when power is applied to one side. Straight-line backing is best accomplished by using a Reverse-C (figure 5-18)—a slightly modified version of the J-stroke done in reverse. In tricky currents an accomplished solo paddler will often alternate between this stroke and a diagonal draw (a conventional draw applied at a 45 degree angle to the canoe).

The Draw Stroke

The draw stroke is the most important turning stroke. A powerful draw makes the bow person an active navigator rather than just a horsepower machine (figure 5-5)

For maximum power the draw should be executed from a kneeling position. Reach out as far from the gunwale as you can—don't be afraid to lean the canoe. Keep your top hand high and draw the paddle quickly and powerfully toward you. When the paddle reaches within 6 inches of the canoe, slice it out and draw again.

Solo Adaptation

Figure 5-5 Draw stroke.

It is important to realize that the force of the water under the canoe has a righting effect on the canoe, so you can lean way out on this stroke and apply power with your whole body. The canoe *will not* tip over. The righting effect ceases, however, when the paddle is no longer in motion, so you must recenter your weight the moment you take the power off the paddle. The modern trend of running rapids is to run them as slowly as possible, as this gives you time to respond correctly and results in less damage to your canoe if it strikes a rock. Rudder motions are useful for turning only if you have forward speed, which is why the draw is so important. Although commonly used by both paddlers, the

Figure 5-6 "Draw...draw!"

DRAW! DRAW!

draw is most effective in the bow. It is not uncommon on whitewater streams to hear off in the distance a desperate stern paddler screaming "Draw...draw!" to a frustrated partner.

Solo adaptations: Identical to the tandem draw. Net movement of the canoe is sideways, in the direction of the stroke. By varying the angle of the draw (to the diagonal), a variety of intriguing moves are possible.

The Pryaway (Pry) Stroke

The pryaway is used for moving the canoe away from your paddling side. It's a modern version of the old "pushover" stroke, though considerably more powerful. Slice the paddle into the water as far under the canoe as possible and with a deft, powerful motion pry the paddle over the bilge. After some practice you'll find that it's easier and faster to use an underwater rather than an aerial recovery for your paddle. The mechanics of this will come naturally after a short time.

Figure 5-7 The Pryaway

CANOEING AND CAMPING

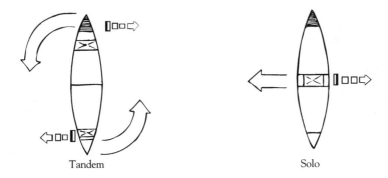

Tandem   Solo

Figure 5-8 The Pryaway: Aerial view of the pryaway for both tandem and solo.

Unlike the draw, the pryaway has no righting effect, so you must keep your weight centered throughout the stroke. Since the pryaway is very powerful, it should not be used in shallow water where the paddle might catch on a rock and overturn the canoe. In shallow water the bow person should use a cross draw.

Solo adaptations: The pryaway is best at home in heavy water (powerful waves) where you need a quick lateral move plus the stability (bracing action) of a paddle that's always in the water. It is an essential stroke in the solo whitewater canoe.

The Cross Draw

The cross draw, as the name implies, is a draw stroke crossed over to the other side of the canoe. It is used in water too shallow to effect a proper pryaway.

Pivot at the waist, swing the paddle over the bow (the stroke cannot be done in the stern)…and *draw!* Don't change your grip on the paddle. Angle the paddle forward so it is nearly parallel to the water. Force water under and in

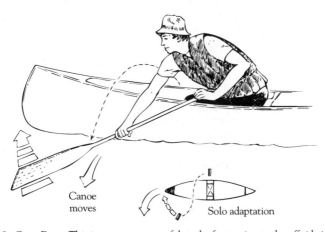

Canoe moves   Solo adaptation

Figure 5-9 Cross Draw: This is your most powerful stroke for turning to the off side in a solo canoe.

front of the bow. As with the pryaway, keep your weight centered, as the cross draw has no stabilizing effect on the canoe.

Solo adaptations: This is THE stroke for turning to the off side in a solo canoe. It is extremely powerful and, if properly applied and coupled with a strong lean, will snap even a straight-keeled solo canoe around quicker than a cat's wink. Older canoe books recommend the "sweep" stroke for off-side turns, but the cross draw is more effective, especially when the canoe has forward motion. Even professional canoe racers who never use crossover maneuvers occasionally cheat and cross draw.

The J-Stroke

A canoe moving forward has a tendency to veer away from the side on which the stern person is paddling. When paddling backward, the reverse is true. The J-stroke is used to keep a canoe on a straight course. It is the stern person's stroke when paddling forward, and a reverse form of it (the reverse J) is used by the bow paddler when moving backward.

Begin the J like a typical forward stroke, but shortly after the paddle enters the water, start changing its pitch ever so slightly by turning the thumb of your top hand down and away from your body. As the paddle is pushed forward through the water, continue to increase the pitch progressively. At the completion of the stroke the thumb of the top hand should be pointing straight down, placing the paddle in a rudder position. If at the end of the stroke additional correction is needed, force the paddle out from the canoe in a prying fashion. If no further correction is necessary, take the paddle out of the water and repeat the stroke.

There are many variations of the J-stroke, and each canoeist develops a style that suits him or her best. Many very good paddlers finish the stroke by prying the paddle shaft off the gunwales or their thighs. Completing the stroke with a pry is frowned upon in some circles since it abuses paddles (and gunwales). However, it is a very efficient form of the J, and most whitewater canoeists use it. Another variation of the J, used almost exclusively by paddlers of decked slalom canoes, is the thumbs-up J. This stroke is begun as a powerful forward stroke; upon completion the thumb of the top hand is turned quickly, snapping the paddle into a rudder position. A fast pry off the gunwales straightens the canoe. The result is a very powerful and relaxing stroke that permits you to paddle long distances without tiring. Some veteran canoeists scoff at this stroke because they believe the mark of a good paddler is the ability to keep a canoe traveling on a straight course without veering. Both the thumbs-up and pry form of the J cause the canoe to veer slightly back and forth as it is paddled.

Many champion whitewater canoeists use the thumbs-up J for paddling their skittish, decked fiberglass boats. When gliding quietly among the lily pads, the traditional J is best. But in heavy rapids and waves the newer, more efficient variations are often better.

Solo adaptations: The traditional J doesn't provide enough leverage to keep a solo canoe on course. You'll have to use the Solo-C (figure 5-18) instead.

START

FINISH: Thumb of top hand is turned down.

Figure 5-10 The J-stroke

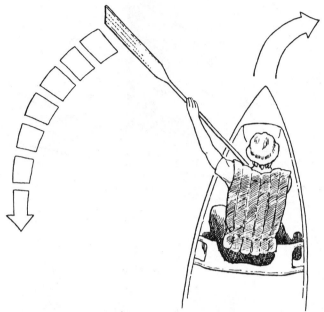

Figure 5-11 The Bow Sweep Stroke

Figure 5-12 The Solo Sweep: Canoe will pivot on its midpoint and turn clockwise.

CANOEING AND CAMPING

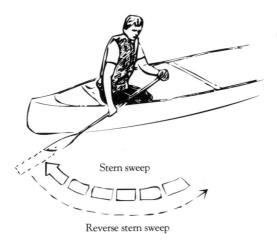

Stern sweep

Reverse stern sweep

Figure 5-13 The Stern Sweep: Canoe will accelerate and turn towards paddler's left.

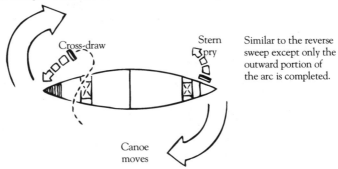

Cross-draw

Stern
pry

Canoe
moves

Similar to the reverse
sweep except only the
outward portion of
the arc is completed.

Figure 5- 14a The Pivot

THE SWEEP STROKES

Sweep strokes are used to turn the canoe in a wide arc, either toward or away from your paddling side. Both the draw and pryaway are more efficient, especially in currents, and if you've mastered these, you will probably reserve the sweeps for quiet-water maneuvers.

Solo adaptions: The "sweep" and "reverse sweep" are essential strokes in the solo canoe and may be used to advantage in currents and heavy water. Use the full sweep in the solo canoe.

The Stern Pry

The stern pry is a powerful stroke for turning the canoe towards the stern person's paddle side. It is similar to the reverse stern sweep except that only the outward portion of the arc is completed. Start the paddle near the tail of the canoe and push it smartly outward. For maximum power pry the paddle shaft off the gunwale

---

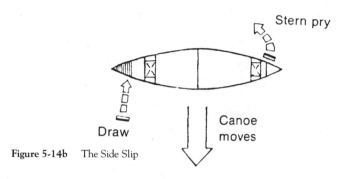

Stern pry

Draw

Canoe
moves

Figure 5-14b   The Side Slip

or your thigh. Combine this stroke with a well-executed cross draw at the bow and the canoe will literally pivot on its midpoint. Use a draw at the bow instead, and the craft will slip sideways (no forward motion) in the direction of the "draw". The "side slip" and pivot illustrated in figures 5-14a and 5-14b are essential whitewater maneuvers.

Note: Because of its long lever arm, the stern pry is more powerful than the pryaway. It is also better in shallow water because the paddle can't catch on rocks and upset the canoe.

The Sculling Draw

The sculling draw is an impressive-looking stroke. It is not one that you need to learn right away, as you can use the draw to perform the same function. However, it is a nice stroke in its place, and that place is in parallel landing to a shoreline in water too shallow to get a good draw.

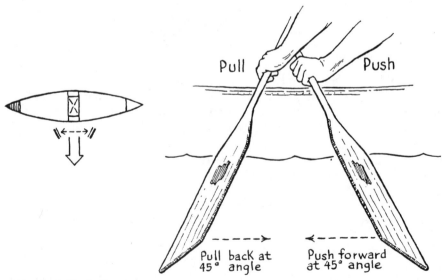

Pull   Push

Pull back at
45° angle

Push forward
at 45° angle

Figure 5-15 The Sculling Draw

CANOEING AND CAMPING

Place the paddle in the water in a draw position at a comfortable distance from the canoe. Turn the leading edge of the paddle about forty-five degrees away from the canoe, and while holding this blade angle pull the paddle backward through the water for a distance of about 2 feet. Then reverse the angle of the leading edge 90 degrees from the previous direction and, while holding this new blade angle, push the paddle forward about 2 feet to complete the stroke. The sculling draw is sometimes called the Figure-8 stroke because the paddle appears to describe an 8 in the water. This is not really accurate, however, since the paddle is pulled straight fore and aft, and only the blade angle is changed.

Figure 5-16 As you gain solo experience, you'll develop a repertoire of special strokes. Here, Phil Sigglekow braces into a turn in his Pat Moore-designed *Proem*. Photo credit: R. Hamilton Smith.

Power Paddling (the "Minnesota Switch")

The term power paddling was coined by Harry Roberts, former editor of *Paddler* magazine. The name describes the dynamic technique in which canoeists paddle powerfully ahead and, on signal, switch sides to maintain a straight course.

About fifty years ago some professional Minnesota racers tried the switching technique in competition. The results were dramatic. Not only could a canoe be paddled faster by switching sides every six strokes or so, but it could be paddled farther since the paddlers became less tired. Over the years the Minnesota switch grew in popularity, and today all professional racers use it instead of the J-stroke.

To an old-school canoeist, the Minnesota switch is a prime example of poor technique, mostly because the canoe does not travel a straight-line course. But it is efficient, especially on wilderness trips when you want to make good time against big oncoming rollers on a windswept lake. Kruger and Waddell used the Minnesota switch almost exclusively on their voyage to the Bering Sea. Their

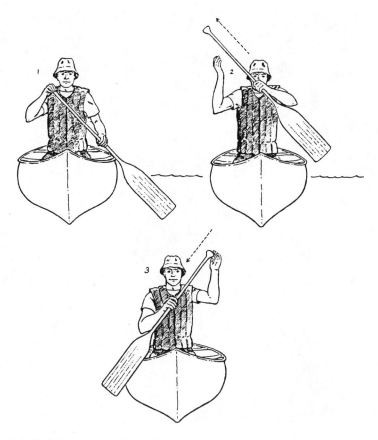

Figure 5-17 The Minnesota Switch: Switching sides is easy as 1,2,3. If correctly done, only a split second is lost.

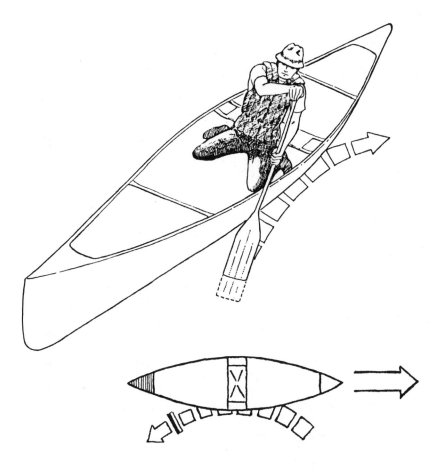

Figure 5-18 The Solo-C. The reverse C (above) is done the opposite of the forward C.

cadence was approximately sixty strokes per minute, with a switch after each six to eight strokes.

 Procedure: Paddlers sit low in the canoe with feet braced (footbraces are desirable) firmly ahead. After a half dozen or so strokes the stern paddler—who can best see the course of the canoe—shouts "HUT"[2] or some other agreed-upon signal. Paddlers then switch sides in unison (see figure 5-17) and without missing a beat, continue to power paddle ahead. This is a precise, snappy maneuver, one

[2]"HUT" is the traditional command for switching paddling sides. It is also the name of the official magazine of the Minnesota Canoe Association.

that requires more finesse and coordination than you might guess. If done correctly, only a split second is lost; if improperly executed in a strong current, a capsize is possible.

Experienced racing teams do all their paddling this way, invariably with bent-shaft paddles. To maneuver, they draw or switch sides and draw—or the bowman uses a "post," which is basically a high brace (figure 5-20). As mentioned, racers occasionally cheat and cross draw at the bow to effect turns. But mostly, they power-paddle ahead and switch sides to maneuver.

Some traditional canoeists maintain that you sacrifice canoe control when you adhere to power-paddling techniques. Until I paddled with the racers, I believed this too. But it simply isn't so. What onlookers often perceive as "loss of control" in tight turns is in reality the maneuvering limits of a racing canoe at speed. Race boats are straight-keeled; at best they turn poorly even when piloted by expert teams. It's doubtful that experienced whitewater folk could make these canoes sing any more beautifully on a twisting course.

However, there's no denying that kneeling paddlers who use long, straight paddles (long paddles have more leverage than short ones) and whitewater slalom strokes in their highly rockered canoes enjoy the greatest control in difficult waters. For this reason the complete canoeist should know—and appreciate—both styles of paddling.

The Braces

Low brace. The low brace functions as an outrigger—it's not really a paddling stroke. Its purpose is to stabilize the canoe in turns and to keep it from capsizing in big waves.

To execute the stroke, reach far out, paddle laid nearly flat on the water, palm of the top hand up. Put your weight solidly on the paddle—a halfhearted effort isn't good enough. If you're capsizing, a powerful downward push will right you. The push should be lightning fast and smooth; don't "slap" the water with your paddle.

The low brace is essential for turning into or out of eddies (see chapter 6, On the Water) and any place the stern person needs to check a strong inside turn. Canoe teams frequently run heavy waves in a "ready brace," or motionless outrigger position. Then, if an unusually high "haystack" (standing wave) threatens to unhorse them, the paddler on the tipping side can instantly brace to offset the dangerous lean.

Solo adaptations: Solo canoes are skittish, and they depend on strong leans and braces to keep them from capsizing in rough water.

You can use the low brace effectively on calm water too. Get up a full head of steam, reach back at about a 30-degree angle, and brace hard, power face of the paddle at a strong climbing angle to the water. The canoe will spin right around your paddle, in effect executing an inside wheelee, or "static axle." Wahoo! Pure fun. The low brace is one of the most important (and spectacular) strokes for playing on quiet water.

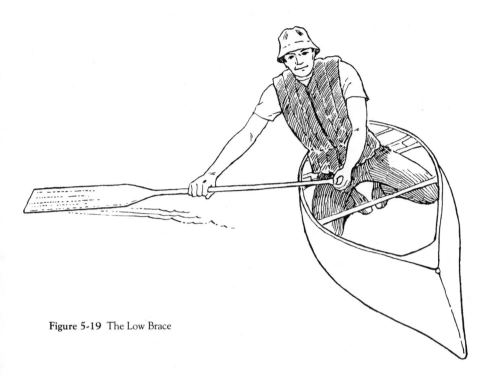

Figure 5-19 The Low Brace

Figure 5-20 The High Brace

High brace. There are times when you need a strong brace, a draw, and a canoe lean all at the same time. Enter the high brace. Basically, the high brace is nothing more than a stationary draw with the power face of the paddle held against the current or at a strong climbing angle to it. The success of the stroke depends on speed—either paddling or current—and a strong lean to offset the pull of the moving water. The high brace blends easily to the draw—an essential stroke for pulling into an eddy and for making sharp turns.

Solo adaptations: When you find yourself capsizing to your off side (side opposite your paddle), reach far out on a high brace and put your weight and trust on your paddle. You cannot do eddy turns or maintain stability in rough water without the high brace!

PADDLING ALONE

See chapter 11, Solo Canoeing Is Different, for what you need to know when paddling solo and tandem canoes alone.

PUREBRED SOLO STROKES

As you've probably already discovered, all the typical tandem strokes can be used with varying success in the solo canoe. There are, however, a number of strokes and techniques that are unique to the solo canoe, and these you'll find detailed in my book *Basic Essentials of Solo Canoeing*, published by ICS Books.

The Solo-C (figure 5-18) is the one purebred solo stroke that you'll want to learn right now. It is nothing more than a refined J-stroke with a diagonal draw component added at the start.

To watch an accomplished soloist C-stroking along, canoe running true and quiet, is a rare treat. Mastery of the Solo-C represents canoe technique at its pinnacle!

LEANING THE CANOE

It would be unfair to leave the subject of paddling without mentioning the technique of leaning the canoe to make a turn. To make a gradual turn with the canoe under power, lean the canoe (an inch or two is sufficient) to the outside of the turn (the reverse of what you would do on a bicycle). If you hold the lean, the canoe will cut a nice arc in the opposite direction of the lean. Professional racers do much of their turning by this method, and lone paddlers of decked slalom canoes often use a counterlean to help keep their skittish boats from turning away from their paddling side. *Caution:* Don't use this technique for quick turns in rapids—you'll upset the canoe!

STANDING IN THE CANOE

The procedures discussed in this chapter naturally assume that you will either sit or kneel in your canoe. But what about standing? Is it a viable position? Older canoe books suggest that it is, while modern texts dismiss the idea with a simple snicker and an admonition that you should "never stand" in a canoe.

Hogwash! There are two times when you may want to stand in your canoe: (1) Just before entering a rapid—to check the course from a higher vantage point, and (2) in calm water when you want to stretch your legs. Those who suggest that standing in a canoe is unsafe simply don't know the limits of their craft. It is, in fact, possible to stand in almost any canoe—even a skittish solo one—if you brace your feet wide apart and maintain balance on the center line.

CHAPTER SIX

On the Water

Once, along the Hood River in the Northwest Territories of Canada, my partner and I entered what appeared to be a relatively simple rapid, only to discover that the waves and hydraulics were much worse than we had bargained for. It required all our strength and skill just to maintain alignment with the powerful current—to keep from capsizing in the frothy water. The waves grew to monster proportions, and ultimately they completely engulfed the canoe and blotted my bowman from sight. But the tough nylon spray cover held, and the big Royalex canoe plunged confidently on through.

The run was a long one, perhaps a quarter mile. There was no time to "question" the route, only react. Finally, it was over and we drifted aimlessly into the pool of ice-blue water below, our faces beaming with smiles, our bodies pumped high with the excitement of a successful run. Granted, we had stepped beyond safe bounds, but we had made it, and through it all we had retained perfect control of our craft (or so we thought). But our friends on shore had quite a different perspective. They laid into us with vociferous threats, unrepeatable expletives, and gave fair warning that we better never, never pull a dumb stunt like that again! Repeated attempts to clear ourselves by suggesting that the run was "easy" was not enough. It was evident to everyone that God had directed our descent. We humbly apologized and vowed to show better judgment "next time."

As you have just observed, luck will occasionally get you through a difficult whitewater passage or across a dangerous running sea, but more often than not a lucky paddler is a good paddler. Unfortunately, in the process of becoming good, a spill or three is inevitable. Although competent canoeists question those who tip frequently, they wonder about those who have never tipped at all. Your safety on a canoe trip depends in large measure on your ability to respond correctly—and automatically—in dangerous situations. Proper responses can only be learned from practice. "Upsetting experiences" have educational value, and your survival in rapids may well depend on your whitewater education.

LOADING THE CANOE FOR ROUGH-WATER TRAVEL

Canoes should be loaded in the water, not on land. Standing in or placing heavy loads in canoes half out of water can bend aluminum and break wood and fiberglass bottoms. Admittedly, there are times when you may have to "bridge" your canoe while loading it. Just be careful, and don't make a practice of this procedure.

A canoe almost always handles better when loaded dead level. Neither the bow nor the stern should be higher. If an uneven distribution of weight is unavoidable, the lesser of two evils is to lighten the bow. But a light bow will give you problems in a head wind—you'll have difficulty keeping on course (the canoe will try to weather-vane into the wind). On the other hand, a weighted stern will provide better directional control in a following sea, although if the tail is too low, big waves may pour right in! In rapids directional control will be reduced by burying one end. With the front end high you may successfully negotiate large, standing waves, but you'll lose this advantage when you pile up on a rock because you can't maneuver. So load dead level whenever possible and keep the weight as close to the center and as low as possible in the canoe.

CATAMARANED CANOES

For greater stability on rough water or while sailing, some authorities recommend that you "catamaran" a pair of similar canoes. To prevent water buildup between the two craft, you are generally advised to use strong poles to separate the canoes about 4 feet at the bow and 6 feet at the stern. If poles are securely lashed to the canoes and a large square sail is hoisted, the rig will make reasonably good time in a strong tail wind. However, running at an angle to the wind (tacking) is nearly impossible with such an outfit, and any degree of maneuverability is out of the question. Moreover, an important advantage of the single canoe over more stable, paired craft is its ability to roll with the side thrust of waves—an ability that is completely negated by the rigid, unyielding design of the catamaran. In short, paired canoes respond poorly to the pitch of a rough sea and consequently tend to ship water readily.

An additional concern is the danger of a rope lashing or wood crossbrace breaking, and if this happens in a good blow, a dunking is inevitable. I have used paired canoes for casual downwind sailing and for placid-water recreational paddling, but I consider them downright dangerous for general rough-water use, with or without sails. A well-designed canoe will weather out 6-foot waves if paddled by a team of experts. Catamaran-rigged canoes, on the other hand, even if securely braced and tied, are almost sure to break apart under these conditions.

When a sudden squall blows up and the waves grow to impressive heights, you will do best to put your faith in proper canoeing techniques. If this fails, hang on to your swamped canoe and trust your life jacket.

CANOE SAILING

On a trip to James Bay we fought wind and driving rain for ten straight days without a break. At one point in the trip we covered only twelve miles in three days without a break. On another day sixteen hours of strenuous, continuous paddling were required to cross twenty-mile-long Mattagami Lake, just south of Smoky Falls, Ontario. When we finally entered the very large Moose River, we knew we would have to fight the prevailing north wind for more than a hundred miles to reach James Bay. Then a miraculous change of weather occurred. The wind shifted completely to the south, providing us with a steady tail wind of perhaps twenty knots. We quickly fashioned sails and put out to sea, easily covering the one-hundred-mile distance to Moosonee in just fifteen hours! Shortly after we arrived at our destination, the wind reversed itself again. Our sail had given us the edge to play the weather odds and win.

The best and easiest way to rig a sail for a wilderness canoe is to use two paddles or poles and a rainfly or poncho. Roll the fly or poncho around the paddles as you would a scroll (figure 6-1). In practice the bow person holds the rig against the gunwales and supports the paddle blades (or pole bases) with his thighs or feet. By opening and closing the scroll-like sail to catch the wind, you can control the speed of the canoe. You can also change the direction of the sail somewhat, allowing you to tack slightly.

It is not a good idea to tie makeshift sails in place on loaded wilderness canoes. A heavily loaded canoe can easily get out of control in a high wind and capsize, throwing you overboard while it keeps on plowing down the lake. You may find yourself not only in the water in a running sea but canoeless as well. Hand-held sails work well enough for most situations. If you prefer a sturdier, more permanent arrangement, install a mast step and bar and do it right.

Figure 6-1   Two paddles and a rain fly or poncho is the easiest way to rig a sail.

EVASIVE TACTICS

Assume you are canoeing on a river with a strong current. Directly in front of your canoe is a large rock. If you try to steer around the rock, you are likely to get caught broadside and possibly destroy your canoe. Back-paddling is not the answer, for that will merely postpone the inevitable. You require a tactic that will slow the canoe down and move it sideways at the same time—you need a back ferry.

The back ferry makes use of two directional forces: the forward velocity of the river and the back-paddling speed of your canoe. In figure 6-2 the stern person is paddling on the left and begins the back ferry with a powerful stern pry. The pry is repeated until the proper angle to the current (usually about 30 degrees) is attained. The stern paddler then joins the bow person in paddling vigorously backward. The net movement, as illustrated, will be nearly sideways. The faster the river speed, the smaller the ferry angle, and vice versa.[3] Only experience will tell you what angle is best. You can easily increase or decrease the ferry angle by drawing or prying as needed.

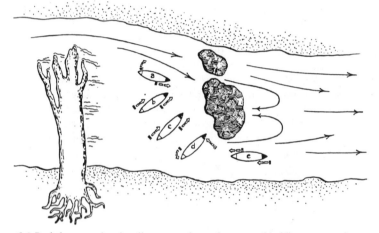

Figure 6-2 Back ferry to safety (small arrows indicate direction of paddle movement).

On powerful, fast-flowing rivers getting to shore quickly can be important, especially if there is a bad rapid or bouldery falls ahead. Begin the back ferry by angling your stern in the direction you want to go. Maintain the proper angle and paddle backward until your stern barely touches the shore. Then pull the bow around (using a draw or pry, whichever is appropriate) until the canoe is parallel to the land.

[3]This relationship becomes reversed when the river speed exceeds your paddling speed. Although there is a definite trigonometric relationship between the speed of the current and the angle you should hold, in heavy rapids there is danger of swamping the canoe if you let your ferry angle get too large (greater than about 40 degrees).

Landing stern first is a good habit to get into. In very swift currents bow landings can be dangerous because a river is slowest near its edges and fastest near its center. When you nose into the slow water at the shoreline, the faster main current grabs your stern and spins it downstream. If there is a sufficient current differential, you can be spun around so rapidly that you may lose your balance and possibly overturn the canoe.

Another evasive tactic based on the principle of vectors is the forward ferry. It is identical to the back ferry except that you spin the canoe 180 degrees and paddle forward instead of backward. This technique is used mostly by paddlers of kayaks and canoes that can turn quickly. Since the forward ferry is considerably more powerful than its backward counterpart, you can use a steeper angle to the current. You can also paddle longer distances without tiring.

On a recent Canadian river trip my partner and I put ashore just above a bouldery falls. After about an hour of scouting we concluded that portaging was out of the question because a high rock bluff ran for several hundred yards along the river's edge. It was apparent that a portage, if one existed, was on the other bank of the 100-yard-wide river. Somehow we would have to cross to the other side. We were within 50 feet of the falls, and the current was moving at perhaps five miles per hour. Paddling straight across was out of the question. We decided to use a very shallow-angled forward ferry to test the current. Encountering no difficulty at the outset of our crossing, we steepened the angle considerably as we approached the center. We landed almost directly opposite our starting point on the other side of the river. I don't know what we would have done if this method had been unknown to us.

Although there are other whitewater techniques, wilderness canoes are usually heavily loaded and thus respond very sluggishly to the paddle. You can't effectively draw a heavy canoe sideways very far to avoid obstacles. Ferrying will be one of your most useful river tactics.

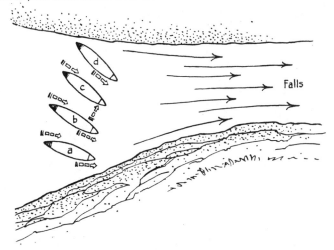

Figure 6-3 Crossing a river using a forward ferry (arrows indicate direction of paddle movement).

RIVER FEATURES

River Bends

Whenever possible, stay on the inside of all bends. Rivers run fastest and deepest at the outside bends, and because of this most of the debris usually piles up there. Should you overturn and get your life jacket or clothing caught in the branches of a half-submerged tree, it could be impossible to work your way free. You may be lucky to escape with your life! For this reason you should seek the outside of a bend only when the water is low or the current sluggish.

The safest way to negotiate bends is by ferrying. For crossing wide expanses of water the forward ferry is preferred; otherwise, the back ferry is best. To begin the back ferry as you approach a curve, tuck your tail to the inside of the bend and back-paddle. Although going around a bend sideways appears dangerous, it is in fact quite safe, for your canoe is almost perfectly aligned with the current. A slight pry or draw will quickly spin the bow downstream, putting you back on course. When you hear the thunder of rapids ahead but a curve prevents your seeing the telltale "haystacks," get to the inside of the bend and cautiously back ferry, keeping your stern just a few feet from shore. Should the rapid prove unrunnable, a few paddle strokes will bring you to the safety of the river bank.

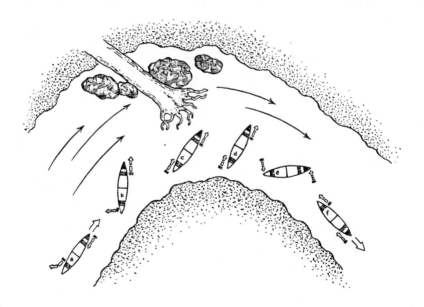

Figure 6-4 Ferrying Around a Sharp Bend: Keep away from the outside of the bends, except in low water (arrows indicate direction of the paddle movement).

In 1982 friends and I experienced a polar gale along the remote Hood River in Canada's Northwest Territories. For three days we were confined to our tents by fifty-five-mile-per-hour winds and unrelenting rain. When the weather cleared, we were greeted by a silt-choked river in flood stage, the hydraulics of which were unbelievable. There were uprooted dwarf willows and debris everywhere in the river, and they all piled up on the outside curves. The powerful current, which we estimated at more than ten miles an hour, produced man-sized waves at the outside of every bend. In many places the river was more than a quarter mile wide!

Getting downstream that day was a matter of staying tight on the inside bends, away from the debris and engulfing whitewater. First we would ferry furiously to reach a right bank, only to ferry back across the channel when the river curved left. It was a continuous and exhaustive battle to stay on the inside curves. And it would have been impossible without our well-practiced ferries. Indeed, I doubt if we could have gotten downriver without them!

A final note on ferrying: Early in this chapter I emphatically suggested that canoes should always be trimmed dead level. Ferrying is an exception. Here, the downstream end is best trimmed slightly down. Since it's usually impractical to lighten one end of the canoe before the start of the ferry, your best bet is to always load dead level!

Eddies Are a Canoeist's Friend

If you have ever thrown a stick just beyond a large rock or bridge piling in a river with a good current, you have probably observed that the stick floats back upstream in the lazy current below the obstacle. This is an eddy. Paddling long stretches of difficult rapids can be exceedingly nerve-racking. The quiet water of an eddy is a convenient stopping place to rest and collect your thoughts. Polers commonly travel upstream by hopping from eddy to eddy. If the water is sufficiently deep, paddlers can also successfully use this technique.

Since the movement of water within an eddy is opposite to that of the river's flow, there is a current differential at the eddy's edge. This is the *eddy line*, and crossing it in strong currents can be dangerous if you are not prepared for the consequences. If you cautiously poke your bow into the slow upstream current, the main flow of the river will catch your stern and spin it quickly downstream. The result is a possible dunking. To enter an eddy bow first, you must drive powerfully forward across the eddy line. As the stern swings downstream, lean the canoe upstream to prevent upsetting. In figure 6-5a the bow person "hangs on" to the calm water of the eddy with a strong high brace and a severe lean, while the stern person—who has not yet crossed the eddy line—also leans to the right to offset the centrifugal force of the current. As soon as the canoe completes the turn (which takes only a split second), the pair paddles forcefully up to the rock.

If, however, the bow person were paddling on the left (figure 6-5b) and the stern person on the right, the roles—but not the canoe lean—would be reversed. Both paddlers would drive the canoe forward until it crossed the eddy line; then, at that moment, the stern person would lean far out on a low brace while the bow person sliced forward into the eddy, completing the maneuver with a pry and a forward drive. Whew!

Figure 6-5a An Eddy Turn with a High Brace in the Inside: Canoe must be leaned *upstream* when the bow crosses the eddy line.

Figure 6-5b An Eddy Turn with a Low Brace on the Inside: Bow person may use a pry, as illustrated (preferred) or a cross draw to turn the canoe into the eddy.

Figure 6-6 The Peel-Out: Canoe enters the current at about a 45-degree angle. Bow paddler uses a high brace and leans the canoe downstream as the bow crosses the eddy line.

Figure 6-7 The Peel-Out: Using a low brace on the downstream side, the bow paddler stabilizes the canoe with a a pry (illustrated) or a cross draw as the current spins it downstream.

Whenever possible, I prefer to "eddy in" with the bow paddle on the inside of the turn as illustrated in figure 6-5a. The procedure is less tricky and seems to result in greater control due to the powerful stabilizing effect of the high brace up front.

Any eddy turn from a fast current is exciting and sure to produce a dumping if you aren't well-practiced in the technique. The most common error is failure to apply a strong upstream lean as the eddy line is crossed. Another mistake is that of judgment—entering the eddy too late. It won't take you long to discover that you'll miss the eddy by a wide margin unless you enter it just below the rock. The current carries you downstream, remember?

All this talk about bow-first eddy turns is academic, for the sluggish response of heavily laden touring canoes generally precludes effective use of the technique except in weak or moderate currents. The safest way to enter an eddy is by back ferrying. Begin the ferry as you approach the eddy line. Set the stern into the quiet water and paddle back to safety. When you have rested sufficiently, leave the eddy at its weak lower end. If the upstream current is very strong, this may be impossible, in which case you'll have to use a fast forward ferry combined with a strong downstream lean—a sophisticated tactic called the "peel-out."

To do a peel-out, the canoe is angled at least 45 degrees to the current (a somewhat steeper angle than is used for ferrying) and forward power applied. As the bow crosses the eddy line, the bow person reaches far out on a high brace and leans the canoe downstream (figure 6-6). The stern supports the lean and "sweeps" the canoe around. As the boat realigns with the current, the pair recenters the weight and resumes normal paddling.

In the alternative method (figure 6-7) the bow person paddles on the left and the stern person on the right. As the bow crosses the eddy line, both partners lean downstream; the bow person pries or crossdraws while the stern person applies a low brace.

Here again I prefer the former practice (high brace on the inside of the turn), as it seems to provide greater stability as the bow crosses the eddy line. But perhaps I'm simply more experienced in the procedure.

When paddling difficult rapids, you should proceed from eddy to eddy. At each new stopping place you can survey the conditions ahead and determine the safest course. Eddies can be used to your advantage only if you can perform competent ferries, so the importance of these tactics cannot be overemphasized!

Chutes

When the river narrows sufficiently for its flow to be severely restricted, a chute of whitewater is formed. When the fast water racing through the chute reaches the calmer water below, its energy dissipates in the form of nearly erect standing waves called haystacks. A series of uniform haystacks indicates deep water and safe canoeing—that is, if they are not so large as to swamp the canoe. To help the bow lift over the large haystacks, you can slow the canoe's speed by back-paddling or you can quarter into the waves at a slight angle. You can also lighten the front end by putting the bow paddler behind the seat. Running a chute with large standing waves below is one of the few times when you may wish to stop and rearrange the load in your canoe.

Falls and Dams

Low falls can be successfully run if there is sufficient water flowing over them and if they are not so steep as to produce a heavy back roller at their base. If after checking a falls you decide it is safe to run, pick the point of strongest water flow, align the canoe, and proceed at river speed over the falls. Upon reaching the base of the falls, dig your paddles hard and deep to climb out of the trough below.

It is almost always unsafe to run a dam—any dam, even a low one—unless, of course, part of it has broken away. The trouble with dams is not the lack of flow over them or even the steepness of their drops. Rather, the danger lies in the well-formed back roller at their bases. The back roller is actually an extremely powerful eddy, and the upstream current of this eddy can stop you dead in your tracks. Your canoe can be flipped broadside to the current and may spin over and over like a rolling cigar, perhaps to remain trapped until a period of drought lowers the volume of the river. Because some ledges and falls produce the same effects as dams, they should be considered extremely dangerous until proven otherwise.

Choosing a Safe Course Through Rapids

Negotiating a complex rapid without incident requires skill, cool determination, an accurate appraisal of the dangers, and a good partner! Here are the rules for safe passage:

1. An *upstream* vee indicates the location of rocks (figure 6-8); a *downstream* vee is the safe approach.
2. You can't steer around obstacles in a fast-moving river. Rely instead on ferry techniques or side-slip maneuvers (the bow person draws while the stern person pries, or vice versa).
3. Scout the rapids from shore before you run them, and view everything from a downstream vantage point. Often, a substantial drop (ledge) that is invisible from above will be immediately evident from below. A binocular (not a monocular!) is useful for checking questionable spots.
4. Proceed downstream slowly—back-paddle to reduce speed. Maintain control with effective draws, prys, crossdraws, and ferry techniques.
5. Take advantage of eddies to recover your strength and plan your strategy for the water ahead.

After years of teaching whitewater skills, I remain unconvinced that you can learn to read whitewater—to choose a safe course through rapids—from reading books. Certainly, you can learn the important paddle strokes and procedures, but that's not enough. Studying whitewater tactics on a printed page is akin to poring over a map of Great Slave Lake, only to discover its harsh realities from the seat of your canoe. If you want to become proficient at reading

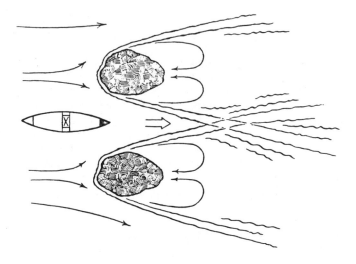

Figure 6-8 Choose a safe "downstream vee" when entering a rapid.

and running whitewater, you'll have to paddle in it—or more accurately, "play" in it. A weekend of on-the-water practice in the company of paddlers who understand the ways of running water will teach you more about choosing a safe course through rapids than a winter of fireside reading.

A WORD ABOUT YOUR PARTNER

Some canoeists are lucky enough to paddle with the same partner all the time. Others are less fortunate; they have to adjust to the ways and incompetencies of a new person on every trip they take. Whitewater training sessions? Are you kidding? Learning comes out of necessity in the course of the canoe trip! By trip's end the new man or woman is "trained." Too bad that we may never see him or her again! All of which brings us to the ultimate bottom line: **White water tactics are for practiced whitewater teams. If in doubt about your partner's ability, portage, portage, portage!**

Early in my paddling career I discovered that the best way to train a new partner was to make all route decisions (and shout commands!) from my position in the stern—a practice complicated by the fact that the person up front is closer to the obstacles and can therefore see them much better. So I developed the habit of angling the canoe about 45 degrees to the current whenever I ran rapids. This improved visibility tremendously and enabled me to make more accurate judgments. A quick draw or pry instantly put the canoe back in alignment with the flow. Drifting at an angle to the current had another advantage; the boat was correctly set up for an immediate back ferry. To avoid a rock dead ahead, I'd simply call, "Back," and the canoe would respond with sideward motion.

CANOEING AND CAMPING

Running angled also has the net effect of shortening the waterline of the canoe, which, like "quartering" lake waves, translates into a drier ride. Negotiating rapids out of alignment to the current is common practice among the experienced North Woods guides, although the value of the technique is seldom expounded in the canoeing literature.

HEAVY WATER

Heavy water is defined as rapids that generally rate high Class III or better (see the AWA River Rating Scale below). Here, waves rise to impressive heights with deep canoe-engulfing troughs below. Where large volumes of water flow over big surface rocks, a "hydraulic jump," or eddy set on edge appears. This is the "sousehole"—a playground for decked whitewater canoes manned by expert paddlers, but no place for open canoes, no matter how skilled their occupants. (Amazingly, souse holes have been negotiated by skilled paddlers in open canoes.)

Negotiating huge waves, powerful currents, and boiling eddies calls for skill, iron-tough nerves, specialized equipment, a good partner, and a philosophy different from that of the cautious slower-than-the-current (back-ferrying and back-paddling) procedures I've outlined. When waves grow to human size and the trough below threatens to swallow you up, you must shift into high gear—paddle forward with gusto so as to have sufficient momentum to climb the faces of the big waves. Even then a swamping may be inevitable unless your canoe has plenty of speed and a fabric splash cover.

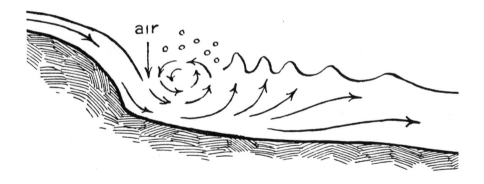

Figure 6-9 Souse Hole: The air-filled back roller of a souse hole can swamp a canoe and trap it. To escape, you must swim out the side of the hole or shed your life vest and dive below the foam into the bottom current—procedures that require skill and determination. Souse holes are no place for open canoes.

Heavy water is something you should look at, reverently photograph, then confidently portage around!

Many of the new guide books rate rapids according to the AWA (American Whitewater Affiliation) International River Rating Scale. This is most handy, as it allows you to plan a trip with confidence. In guide books where this rating scale has not been followed, you must rely on the individual judgment of the writer, which may be considerably different than your own. The International River Rating Scale is the great equalizer.

AWA INTERNATIONAL RIVER RATING SCALE

Water Class and Characteristics

I. EASY—Bends without difficulty, small rapids with waves regular and low. Obstacles like fallen trees, bridge pilings, and so on. River speed less than hard back-paddling speed.

II. MEDIUM—Fairly frequent but unobstructed rapids with regular waves and low ledges. River speed occasionally exceeding hard back-paddling speed.

III. DIFFICULT—Small falls; large, regular waves covering boat. Expert maneuvering required. Course not always easily recognizable. Current speed usually less than fast forward-paddling speed. (Splash cover useful.)

IV. VERY DIFFICULT—High, powerful waves and difficult eddies. Abrupt bends and difficult broken water. Powerful and precise maneuvering mandatory. (Splash cover essential.)

V. EXCEEDINGLY DIFFICULT—Very fast eddies, violent current, steep drops.

VI. LIMIT OF NAVIGABILITY—Navigable only at select water conditions by teams of experts. Cannot be attempted without risk of life.

For all practical purposes a loaded wilderness canoe should not be taken into rapids of a higher classification than II. The risks are just too great. You should realize that a heavy spring rain can turn mild Class I rapids into wild Class IIs or IIIs and an early fall drought can tame a Class III to where you can walk right down the middle of it. Water levels are extremely important in sizing up rapids. Where gauging stations exist, interpretive information can be secured from the administrative unit responsible for the gauge. This is usually the U.S. Army Corps of Engineers, the U.S. Weather Bureau, or your state's department of natural resources or conservation.

Your most accurate information, however, will be available from local canoe clubs that maintain their own gauges. These can be anything from a paint mark on a bridge piling to a rusted pipe. Primitive though they are, club gauges reflect the needs of canoeists and thus are most useful.

LINING AND TRACKING

One morning, after some two hours of leisurely paddling down Ontario's Moose River, my partner suddenly realized that he had left his three-hundred-dollar camera at our last campsite. Somewhat begrudgingly and with unrepeatable expletives, I grabbed a painter and helped him tow the canoe seven miles upstream to our island campsite of the night before. I doubt that we could have paddled that distance very easily.

Upstream tracking is useful not only for retrieving lost cameras but also for getting around rapids when a portage is difficult or impossible to make. For best results while tracking, the upstream end of the canoe should be kept up. If your towing link or ring is located very far above the waterline, you will have to disconnect the bow rope and rig a towing harness. You want the line pulling right from the keel, if possible. The stern line is less important and can remain at its usual place of attachment.

Upstream tracking is just like ferrying. By keeping the canoe at a slight angle to the current (bow out, stern toward shore) while towing, you can walk upstream along the bank and the wash of the current will carry the canoe out to the center of the river. Changing the angle of the canoe while pulling on the ropes will return it to shore. Obviously, tracking is impossible if shorelines are to brushy or rugged to walk along.

The opposite of tracking is lining. This procedure is considerably more common than upstream work and is widely used to get around small falls, ledges, and other obstacles in the river. Some authorities recommend attaching lines to keep the upstream end of the canoe raised. They also advise attaching the bow line to a gunwale near the seat. I have found it best to leave lines attached to their customary rings at the bow and stern (which should be located close to the waterline). Often, while lining, you will be working above the canoe or, possibly, hopping from rock to rock, sometimes pulling from different sides of the canoe. If, for example, you let the canoe down a chute and for some reason need to pull it back up to realign it with the main current, you will be at a serious disadvantage if your lines are attached anywhere other than at the ends.

Canoeing texts make lining sound easy. It isn't! Controlling the path of a heavily loaded canoe in the powerful side-wash of a rock-studded passage requires practice. And agility! The recommended procedure is to use lines at both bow and stern. However, coordinating two ropes—and two people—requires much more skill than you might believe. Even the smallest miscalculation can send the canoe reeling sideways where it may fill with water and wrap neatly around a rock or be broken nicely in two. For this reason many experienced canoeists prefer to line their canoe alone, with a single tail rope, even though it results in some loss of control.

WHITEWATER SAFETY

Despite some dangers inherent in the sport of canoeing, it is essentially a safe pastime. Whitewater clubs take to the rivers as soon as the ice melts, and although the water temperature is very cold (sometimes just a few degrees above freezing), we seldom hear of a drowning. This is because experienced paddlers respect the rivers and are well prepared for upsets. Herein lies the key to whitewater safety: *Be prepared for an upset!*

Life Jackets

Many beginners assume that being a good swimmer is the most important safety consideration. While swimming ability is important, a life jacket and a cool head are more important. Except in unusually calm conditions, you should wear your life jacket at all times. On a wilderness trip, especially, you are burdened with the extra weight of heavy clothes and boots. An upset in even a moderate rapid or mildly choppy lake can be hazardous. Lack of a life preserver has accompanied almost every canoeing fatality.

In 1974 a canoeist lost his life on the Coppermine River in the Northwest Territories of Canada. The man was a good swimmer and an experienced whitewater paddler. He and his partner put ashore just above a difficult rapid known as Rocky Defile. After considerable scouting, the pair decided to run the rapid. As soon as they started downstream, the canoeist realized that he was not wearing his life jacket. He had taken it off while checking the rapids and had neglected to put it back on. But it was too late. The canoe nosed into a heavy roller and began to climb. When it reached the top of the large wave, it teetered and flipped over on its side, throwing both paddlers out of the canoe. Four weeks later the body of the unfortunate canoeist was found. His partner, who wore a life jacket, survived and completed the remaining two hundred miles of the journey alone. It is ironic that in the many miles these experts had paddled together, this was the first time that either had neglected to wear his life jacket. It was not

Figure 6-10 Type III Style Life Jacket (vertical ribbed): Get a life jacket that does not interfere with swimming!

Figure 6-11 Type III Style Life Jacket (panel style).

CANOEING AND CAMPING

incompetence that cost the life of this canoeist, rather, it was an oversight—a simple procedural omission—like forgetting to buckle your seatbelt before you drive. Wilderness rivers bear no malice toward unprepared paddlers; neither, however, do they grant immunity from error.

Because your life jacket is so important, you should select a model that you can wear comfortably all the time. Eliminate from consideration the bulky orange horse-collar type—they are too confining and chafe the neck badly. Choose instead a vertical-ribbed or panel-style vest filled with PVC or polyethylene foam. And don't choose a personal flotation device (PFD) on the strength of Coast Guard approval tags alone. The life-jacket requirements of whitewater paddlers are not the same as those of powerboaters. For example, the proper procedure for swimming in rapids is as follows: Lie on your back, feet pointing downstream. Keep your feet high to prevent somersaulting in the current, and use your feet and canoe paddle to ward off rocks. Swim on your back or side, at an angle to the current, to reach shore. This technique is similar to the canoeist's back ferry.

To do this, you need as much flotation on your back as on your chest, and the bulky horse collars offer virtually no back flotation. Horse collars are designed to float the wearer head up for extended periods of time—at the expense of maneuverability. You are seldom in the water for more than five minutes in a typical canoe upset. In order to avoid obstacles you need a jacket that does not interfere with swimming. Fortunately, the Coast Guard now realizes that the needs of canoeists are best met with Type III flotation devices,[4] which are

Figure 6-12 Safest Way to Swim a Rapid: Keep your feet high to prevent somersaulting in the current, and use your feet and paddle to ward off rocks.

[4]These must keep a conscious person in a vertical or slightly backward position. Adult vests must have a minimum of 15.5 pounds of buoyancy; 11 pounds for medium child's sizes, and 7 pounds for small children. Many Type III PFDs feature much more buoyancy than this.

comfortable to wear for long periods of time. Here's how to test the fit of a life vest that catches your fancy:

Ride-up: Grasp the jacket by the shoulders and lift it upwards until the fabric jams under your armpits. This simulates performance in water. Now turn your head right and left. You should be looking over your shoulder, not at fabric-encased foam. Does the V-neck of the vest crunch against your chin? If so, keep shopping. PFDs that force the chin up may have a more positive righting movement than those that don't, but they hinder maneuverability in water—exactly what you don't want when you have to swim a rapid!

Arm function: Take a seat. This test won't work while standing or kneeling. Now, work your arms vigorously in a paddling motion. Any vest that chafes under the armpits will be intolerable to wear over the long haul.

Flexibility: Hold your arms chest high and draw them smartly inward as far as possible. Does the vest bunch up in front and cramp arm motion? If so, keep looking!

As you shop around for the ideal life vest, you'll learn that sizing, cut, and flexibility vary widely from manufacturer to manufacturer. For this reason it's best **not** to buy a PFD by mail. The above tests are your best indication of good performance in water and a fit you can live with.

It is interesting to note that there is little relationship between your weight out of water and your weight in water. Prospective buyers of life jackets assume that a two-hundred-and-fifty-pound man needs more flotation than a one-hundred-and thirty-pound teenager. If the man is overweight and the teenager is mostly muscle, quite the opposite may be true. It is not uncommon for children to need as much flotation as their parents. Manufacturers have done an excellent job providing properly sized life jackets. The important thing, however, is to realize that the buoyancy rating of the jacket may or may not meet your requirements. You should test your life jacket in both calm water and rapids to assure that it will adequately support you.

KEEPING WARM

Most canoeists rely on polypropylene, pile, or wool garments for warmth. These fabrics won't substitute for a wetsuit in near freezing water, but they will keep you cozy in an all-day rain. As Table 6-2 shows, your body will remain functional in cold water for only a short time. Even this doesn't tell the whole story, because the initial shock of cold water on your chest saps much of your energy. A waterproof paddling shirt can reduce this shock somewhat, but only a wetsuit can eliminate it completely.

Although your body may remain functional for several minutes in cold water, you can die from immersion hypothermia after you've been rescued. Hypothermia occurs when body temperature drops below 95 degrees Fahrenheit. As blood is rushed to the vital organs, chilling spreads throughout the body. This is accompanied by clumsiness, slurred speech, and loss of judgment. Coma and death may occur within a few hours if body temperature is not raised.

Field treatment for someone who has fallen into ice-cold water consists of warming the victim as quickly as possible. If a fire is available, use it! If not, place

Table 6-2

Water Temperature	Amount of Time Body Will Remain Functional
Less than 40 degrees F.	Less than 10 minutes
40 to 50 degrees F.	15 to 20 minutes
50 to 60 degrees F.	15 to 40 minutes
60 degrees F. and above	One or more hours

the naked (skin-to-skin contact) victim into a sleeping bag with one or two people.

If the victim is conscious and can swallow, you may give hot chocolate or soup as a psychological boost. Do not administer stimulants such as coffee or tea.

If hypothermia results from slow chilling over time, the victim should be warmed *gradually*. Apply radiant heat from a fire slowly, or use the classic "sleeping-bag treatment." Through it all, handle the victim gently, as roughhousing may initiate ventricular fibrillation of the heart...and death could result!

A final note: Victims of hypothermia are almost always unaware of the seriousness of their situation. They will continually proclaim, "I'm okay!" It's up to you to diagnose the problem—and treat it quickly!

In 1980 I led a group of teenagers on a trip into the Boundary Waters Canoe Area. There was an icy drizzle and light wind on Saganaga Lake when we put in that morning—nothing serious, just fair warning to dress warm and wear rain clothes. Within the hour the rain picked up. But the kids were all singing and having a grand time, so I saw no reason to put ashore.

As we rounded a point, we overtook another group that was paddling in dead silence. "How's it goin'?" I called encouragingly. Groans of displeasure followed. I paddled alongside the lead canoe and struck up a conversation with the leader.

"Some of these kids don't have good rain gear," he commented. "But they're tough; they can hack it. Besides, we'll be in camp within the hour."

"I dunno," I responded. "Your passenger (a teenage girl) doesn't look so good."

"How ya doin', Linda?" he questioned. "You wanna go ashore and change clothes?"

"I'm okay," she whimpered softly. "I can make it 'til we camp."

The youngster didn't look very well at all. Her lips were blue and she shivered constantly. She had no seat cushion to protect her from the cold, wet bottom of the aluminum canoe. It was a perfect setup for hypothermia.

"I think we'd better get those clothes changed now," I quipped. "C'mon, let's put ashore on that point."

There was another round of "I can make it" from the girl and "These kids are tough" from the leader, but I was insistent, so he finally routed the crew to shore.

The seriousness of the situation became evident when the leader observed that Linda could not get out of the canoe without help. Her legs simply refused to support her body! While we set up the tent and pulled sleeping-bags and dry clothing from packs, the kids crowded around the girl and hugged her to provide as much warmth as possible. Then two girls ushered her into the tent and administered the classic sleeping-bag treatment.

Within the hour Linda was revitalized. But the group decided to remain ashore for the remainder of the day—a wise decision, as hypothermia is a very draining experience, one that requires plenty of rest to fully recover from.

You don't need to paddle a remote wilderness to encounter an episode of hypothermia. People have died while canoeing familiar streams near their home! You have a moral responsibility to use your knowledge of hypothermia to help others you meet in the wilderness. It is not bad manners to strongly suggest that a group bivouac because one member is too cold or too tired to go on. The most inexcusable act you can commit in the outdoors is to say and do nothing when you know there's a possibility that another human being may become injured or die. A human life is an unfair price to pay for ignorance!

BASIC PRECAUTIONS

When you are canoeing whitewater, avoid long coats, ponchos, or anything dangling around your neck on a string. Should you overturn, these items are likely to be caught on submerged tree limbs or between rocks.

Also, avoid heavy boots, and *never* wear waders while paddling. Water-filled waders can make swimming in even a moderate current impossible.

If you overturn, your best life preserver is the canoe, and you should stay with it unless doing so will endanger your life.[5] Upon upsetting, swim immediately to the upstream end of the canoe. A water-filled canoe weighs more than a ton, and should you get between it and a rock, you will be crushed. Hang on to the grab loop or stern painter and try to swim the canoe to shore. The canoe-over-canoe rescue touted by the Red Cross and Scouts works well on calm lakes with empty canoes, but cannot be done with loaded canoes on fast water. Unfortunately, this is where most canoe upsets occur.

[5]If the water is very cold and there is no support crew to come to your rescue, your best bet is to leave the canoe immediately and strike out for shore. Hanging hopefully to a canoe in near freezing water when there is no chance of rescue only hastens your early demise. Contrary to popular belief, and the writings of some canoe authorities, it is not easy to swim a swamped canoe to shore. And if you rely on the action of wind or currents to bring the craft (and you) to land, you're in for a much longer wait than you can afford!

CHAPTER SEVEN

Common Canoeing Hazards

Quick, what's the most dangerous thing about canoeing? If you said "capsizing in a dangerous rapid or in ice-cold water far from shore," you're only partially right. Granted, these "upsetting experiences" occasionally take lives, but more often than not they simply teach respect for the river and then allow the pride-drenched paddlers to continue on their way.

The canoeing literature is filled with pat solutions for negotiating complex rapids and the ice melt of early spring. But what's the rule when you're caught on open water and lightning is striking all around? How should you negotiate the incoming breakers of an open-water expanse? What's the procedure when a following sea planes your canoe to surfing speed? Then there's the threatening business of being tossed about by the powerful waves of motorboat wakes—or worse, of being sandwiched between two of them!

These common hazards seldom cost lives. But they can be terribly frightening, even when you know the rules. Following are the tenets of survival:

LIGHTNING

First scenario: You're paddling along a lakeshore when a storm blows up. Soon, wind-whipped waves send you scurrying along at what seems to be phenomenal speed. No problem... yet! Then you see it—wisps of lightning dancing in the sky. Better get to shore fast! A canoe on open water is no place to be in an electrical storm. The problem is that huge boulders line the shore as far as you can see. Dash into those boulders and you'll pack your canoe home in pieces. The alternative is to keep on paddling and take your chances on being targeted by a million volts of electricity.

Figure 7-1

As you can see, the off-quoted advice to get off the water when lightning strikes is sound only if the shoreline provides both an easy landing and a safe haven from the storm. In our scenario it does neither. Better to stay on open water, *relatively close to land*. Here's why: A lightning-protected zone extends from the tops of the tallest trees (or other topographic features) outward about 45 degrees in all directions. Paddle within this safe "cone of protection" but not so close to its center that lightning may jump from a tree to you. Lightning can easily breach 10 or 20 feet, so—except in unusual circumstances—two or three canoe lengths offshore is the safest place to be.

Second scenario: You're canoeing a small river when the electrical activity begins. Should you head for shore or take your chances on the water? Here, again, your choice should depend on the nature of the adjacent shoreline. For example, south-facing slopes encourage the growth of fast-growing shade-intolerant trees over slower growing ones that can live in shade. This means that some of the tallest trees may stand near the waterway. Holding hopefully to a tall tree is not the safest place to be in a lightning storm! I saw a classic example of this on a small Ontario river some years ago.

The storm began with heavy rain, punctuated by unrelenting lightning. I gathered my teenage crew around me and told them to hang tight and stay well out in the river. As I was explaining the rationale, I saw my colleague's red canoe disappear into the supposed safety of the alder-choked shoreline. Then came the cannon-crack of thunder and the acrid aroma of ozone. Above my friend's head the top of a tall birch was aflame. The red canoe reversed power just as the burning top came crashing down.

As you can see, a tall shoreline tree is no place to be when lightning strikes all around. It is far safer to take your chances on the water, *within the cone of protection*.

Note: There's a misconception that wood and fiberglass canoes are safer than aluminum ones in a lightning storm. No way! A lightning strike may generate millions of volts of electricity—enough to fry anything in its path! The

CANOEING AND CAMPING

fact is that aluminum canoes may actually dissipate current better than nonmetal ones (the charge may be conducted around the hull, into the water). This is all scientific conjecture, you understand!

SURFING IN A FOLLOWING SEA

For a while you are powered along by a gently following breeze. Simply rudder and go with the flow. Then the wind intensifies and you pick up speed. Now the canoe feels lightheaded and out of control, like a monkey on a rubber band. Suddenly, there's a surge of power as the craft peaks a wave and begins to surf. Back paddle and you'll capsize for sure. Continue to rudder and you may do the same. On the other hand, if you can get up enough forward speed to climb off the wave face, the surf may pass you by. At any rate, it's worth a try.

Fortunately, canoes seldom surf very well for very long. Invariably, the wave passes and the stern falls into the trough behind. Whether or not the boat fills with water from the following wave depends on your prowess in climbing up out of the hole. (Just keep paddling and you'll do fine!) Surfing only becomes serious when a rocky shore looms ahead. Then you must get off the wave immediately or be tossed headlong into the boulder line.

To break the surf, get up a full head of steam, then make a snappy, well-braced turn into the wave trough. Lean the canoe smartly away from the oncoming wave. If you pull off the maneuver, you'll gulp some water and stall sideways in the wave trough. If you goof—or lean the wrong way—you'll enjoy a pleasant swim to shore. Once in the trough, simply turn upwind and paddle ashore.

WORKING UPWIND

Working upwind is far safer than going with the flow. All you need to do is keep from taking on water as you knife into the oncoming waves.

Canoeing experts advise you to "quarter" the waves at an approximate 30-degree angle as the bow beats upwind. This procedure shortens the canoe's waterline, making it easier for the craft to fit between waves. The result is greater buoyancy and a drier ride.

However, a canoe on a quartering tack is constantly on the edge of broaching to the wind. The stern person must be in total control. An error here and you'll swim for sure. That's why quartering is a tactic best reserved for experts. Beginners should wipe the technique from their memory banks and instead adopt the "head-on approach."

Procedure: Both partners move closer amidships to lighten the ends of the craft so it will rise and fall more freely with the waves. Point the bow upwind and paddle! Simple as pie. There is no danger of broaching as you power upwind.

MOTORBOAT WAKES

Experienced canoeists often seek out motorboat wakes for the thrill of riding them. Beginners, however, have somewhat cooler feelings towards the experience.

Mix good current with a variable wind, add a speedboat wake, and you have a recipe for a broach, surf, swamping...or all three. Now, introduce the wake from another powerful cruiser and you have the makings for a Class III rapid on your hometown river.

The solution for surviving this mess is to paddle head-on into the maelstrom—not so easy if you're being assaulted from both sides. And if the wave length is short, you may take on water unless you act fast. Pick the closest oncoming wave set and gently paddle straight into it. As the bow rises onto the first roller, angle off into the wave trough (quarter it) to shorten the canoe's waterline length. Keep this gentle quartering course (it gets easier with each passing wave) and you'll stay dry and in command. The opposite wave train you were worried about will be absorbed by the waves in which you are now safely nestled.

Tip: If you see a speedboat bearing full bore your way, raise your hand high, execute a grimace, and give a forceful "thumbs down." More often than not, the boat cuts power on your command.

TOWING

You've finished your canoe trip in a quiet bay of the big lake. Ten miles of open-water travel stretch between you and your car. To save time, you hire a powerboat to tow you to the public landing. What are the safety concerns, if any?

Canoeing texts make towing sound like a lark. Just attach a harness around the canoe so the line pulls right from the keel, run a Y-trace off the powerboat transom (figure 7-2), and speed ahead, worry free.

Don't you believe it!

On calm water a *proper* tow is safe enough. Cruise at moderate speed, make gradual turns—the canoe must not cross the wake path—and you'll have no trouble. However, when the wind comes up, it's a different story. Now, you must balance two variables—waves and the speedboat's wake. Frequently, the two synergize (especially when making turns) and the canoe angles into the wake. The result may be a swamping or capsize and a severely damaged canoe.

The safest way to tow canoes is on an overhead rack built for the purpose. Failing this, you're best advised to wait for calm water—or paddle those ten miles!

TWO IS COMPANY, THREE IS A LOAD!

Some canoeists take canoe capacity recommendations seriously. If the bulkhead sticker reads eight hundred and fifty pounds maximum, half that weight in human cargo should allow for ample freeboard. Or so they think!

First, be aware that manufacturers' load ratings are usually stated to a 6-inch freeboard capacity. Load any canoe that heavy and a few good riffles will sink it at the dock! As mentioned in chapter 1, a 9-inch minimum is more responsible. And movable weight (humans!) juggles all the variables and synergizes everything. Place four ninety-pound teenagers in an eight-hundred-pound-rated canoe and you'll understand. When one kid bounces, the other jounces. The result is an "upsetting" experience.

Obviously, it makes a difference if the human load is seated dead center and on the floor of the canoe. But even then, eight hundred pounds of flour is a more manageable load than half that weight of well-behaved kids. You can improve the odds by substituting grownups for children. But it's still safer to carry the equivalent weight of uncooked pasta!

I've traveled thousands of miles without incident with three in my canoe, and as long as weights are kept reasonable, it's safe enough. Nonetheless, a passenger is always a concern—one that prompts me to portage rapids I'd otherwise paddle with a similar dead-weight cargo aboard. Floatplane pilots frequently "halve" the useful load of their aircraft when carrying a canoe on the pontoons. I suggest you do likewise when you carry a passenger in your canoe!

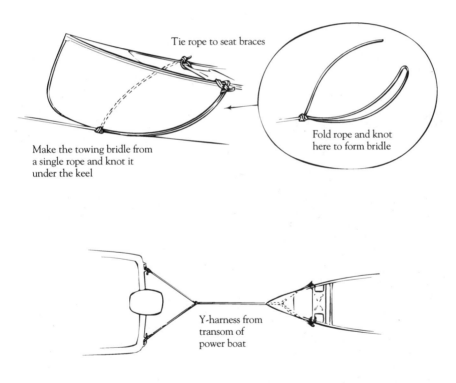

Tie rope to seat braces

Make the towing bridle from a single rope and knot it under the keel

Fold rope and knot here to form bridle

Y-harness from transom of power boat

Figure 7-2 Towing Bridle

CHAPTER EIGHT

Canoe Rescue and Repair

Kettle River—a delightful blend of exquisite scenery and intriguing rapids, a federally protected wild and scenic river that deserves to be. And a favorite playground for Midwestern kayakers and canoers.

Mike and I had made a deal: I'd help him teach the intermediate whitewater course, and he'd provide meals and lodging plus an opportunity to learn some new salvage and rescue techniques developed by the Nantahala Outdoor Center.

My mistake was bringing old Mantoy—a well-used, well-patched, wood-strip solo canoe that friend Bob Brown and I designed. Mantoy had seen tough service on some of the rockiest rivers in Minnesota and Canada, and she had the scars to prove it. Best described as a "nice paddling wreck," Mantoy was just the boat that every whitewater paddler needs to enjoy a river.

Mike watched enviously from shore as I ferried out, eddied in, and did a host of other playful maneuvers, all designed to solicit envy from the crowd. It worked. Mike was jealous; he asked to paddle Mantoy. "Sure," I beamed. "I can paddle solo any time!"

For the better part of the day we practiced in easy Class I-II rapids. The crew gained skill, and by early afternoon they had learned their lessons well enough to begin the "canoe trip."

"Can I take her downriver?" asked Mike, pointing hopefully to the little wood canoe. Before I could answer, he climbed confidently aboard and slipped quietly into the water and out of sight around the next bend.

It was then that I remembered that Mike had the pack with all the rescue gear—the climbing rope, carabiners, pulleys, slings, and the like. Suppose we wrapped a canoe around a midstream boulder? How on earth would we ever get it free?

Well, that wouldn't happen—I'd see to that!

It wasn't a big tree, but it was large enough to command concern. It jutted three-fourths across the river on the inside of a tight hairpin turn. But there was a clear 3-foot channel on the outside—plenty of space for a canoe to scoot through.

My partner and I slipped through the opening, then put ashore to wait for the students and signal them to the outside of the turn. They came through like veterans, first one canoe, then two, then...capsize! Suddenly, there were two paddlers in the grip of the icy water.

Seconds later I saw the comforting sight of two sunlight-yellow life vests skimming the surface. I thanked God that the tree had no submerged branches to entrap the swimmers. I quickly belayed the throwing line around a tree and tossed it out. The woman grabbed it and together my partner and I towed her to shore. Downstream, in the shallows, I observed the man struggling ashore.

The water was a cold 47 degrees Fahrenheit and the air temperature was only slightly warmer. But the flush of excitement had provided a surge of warmth and the pair had not yet begun to shiver. Nonetheless, an immediate change of clothes, hot tea, and affectionate hugs were in order.

And now, to rescue the canoe. The Grumman had bellied-up against the foot-thick log—open end exposed to the full force of the current. Reluctantly, I shuffled along the tree trunk to the pinned canoe. No way could I budge it. "Damn!" I said aloud, "If only we had the proper rescue gear!" But no sense whining; we would have to extract the boat with what we had—100 feet of 3/8-inch nylon rope and one carabiner (an aluminum link through which mountain climbers run their ropes).

The first step was to get a rope around the hull and attached so that it would pull the submerged gunwale up and away from the raging current—a feat of engineering that required the better part of twenty minutes. That accomplished, we rigged a makeshift block and tackle around an upstream tree with a power-cinch (see chapter 10, Tying It All Together) and carabiner. Then everyone pulled...and pulled. No luck.

Next we tried prying the canoe free with a 6-foot length of log. Again, a blank. "Maybe if we pry and winch at the same time," suggested someone. That did it; the gleaming metal hull groaned and popped free like a cookie from a mold. All that remained now was to haul it ashore, dump out the water, and stomp it into a shape that could be paddled.

In this instance salvaging the canoe was no big deal. We could have simply left it and continued downstream in the remaining boats. Later, we could have returned with the rescue equipment. However, had this occurred on a wilderness river, miles from the nearest road, the picture would be much different. Then we could choose between our ingenuity and a long walk home!

EQUIPMENT

If you'll be leading groups down rivers where there's a real possibility that you might have to extract a pinned canoe, then you'd better carry some serious climbing gear—120 feet of Perlon rope, about six carabiners, a couple of nylon pulleys, nylon webbing, and so forth. Otherwise, 100 feet of about 3/8-inch rope, two carabiners, and a rescue pulley should suffice. With these you can rig a two to one (or greater) mechanical advantage pulley over a short distance. If the canoe is hung up so badly that a solid harness, a pry bar, and your best efforts won't get it free, at least wait around for a few days before abandoning it. Rivers often fluctuate greatly from week to week, and an inch or two less water may provide just the edge you need.

If your canoe should ground firmly on a rock in a fast-flowing river and turn broadside to current, the entire side of the craft will be exposed to the force of the rushing water. This force may equal several thousand pounds and may be enough to bend or break the canoe. However, as long as the craft is kept upright, the rushing water will usually pass harmlessly beneath the rounded hull. But if the upstream gunwale should dip below the water and expose the inside of the canoe to the power of the current, the craft may be broken in half or damaged beyond repair. Therefore, it is important that you *never* let the open end of your canoe become exposed to the current. You should make every effort to keep the upstream gunwale up, even if it means leaving your canoe. If necessary, jump into the water on the upstream side of the canoe. Hold tightly to the gunwale and try to work the canoe loose. Usually the removal of your weight is all that's necessary to free the hull. Do not, however, under any circumstances enter the water downstream of the canoe. Should the craft slide off the rock while you are in the water, it could crush you against a downstream obstacle.

REPAIR

Modern canoeists use silver duct (furnace) tape almost exclusively for field repairs of canoes. Duct tape sticks to anything! In fact, canoe owners often neglect more permanent hull repairs simply because furnace tape works so well. A small roll of duct tape should be carried on *all* canoe trips—close to home or otherwise. In thirty-five years of canoeing I have yet to damage a canoe so badly that tape and ingenuity would not repair it.

In the case of aluminum canoes, there is little you can do in the way of field repairs other than apply tape. Where rivets have been pulled, they can be retightened by administering several blows with the back side of an axe. Small gaps and holes can be filled with liquid aluminum epoxy, and these items should be included in your repair kit. Since aluminum canoes usually bend rather than break, physical force will be required to straighten them. An aluminum canoe that has had its gunwales or sides caved in can be placed in shallow water, sand, or mud and stomped back into a semblance of shape. A wood block, the hammer face of an axe, and true grit will produce amazing results.

At home a break in the skin should be repaired by affixing a riveted patch. Complete patch kits available from the Grumman Corporation include patching material, rivets, and instructions. Although a good-quality welding job appears to hold satisfactorily, the aluminum adjacent to the weld may become brittle and cause problems later on. I have seen some fine repair jobs by master aircraft aluminum welders, and these are probably adequate.

Fiberglass, Kevlar, and wood-strip canoes are easily repaired by applying epoxy resin and fiberglass cloth directly to the break. (See my book *Canoeing Wild Rivers* for detailed methods of repairing structural damage.) You can substitute polyester resin for epoxy, but it isn't nearly as strong. (You can patch polyester canoes with epoxy but not vice versa.) Unfortunately, there are dozens of formulations for epoxy and not all are ideal for boat repair. For years I've been using West System epoxy (available from the Gougeon Brothers, Inc., P.O. Box X908, Bay City, MI 48707) and I highly recommend it. This product is as handy as it is strong—unique plastic pumps dispense the correct mix so there's no mess or waste. And West System epoxy kicks solid in temperatures as low as 45 degrees Fahrenheit.

It's unlikely that you'll ever have to repair major damage to a well-built fiberglass or Kevlar canoe. However, you may need to mend chipped gel coat on the "nose" of your canoe after every trip down a shallow rocky stream—easy enough if you *don't* follow the manufacturer's directions. The "book procedure" calls for filling the break with color-matched liquid gel coat, then sanding, buffing, and polishing to blend the repair.

Nothing could be more difficult—or frustrating! Catalyzed liquid gel coat is so runny that it's impossible to contain. The solution is to prop the boat at an awkward angle to "level the flow," then build a well of masking tape around the resin. You then have to nurse the slowly hardening liquid with a flat stick to keep it from overflowing the well. If your patience holds out, the completed patch will hardly be noticeable.

There is an easier way. All you need is a can of white polyester putty (you can substitute gray auto-body putty), which is available at all marinas, and an aerosol can of acrylic enamel or auto lacquer to match the color of your boat.

Procedure:

1. Pick out the shards of damaged gel coat with the blade of your pocket knife.
2. Catalyze the putty (use extra MEKP to produce a "hot" mix) and work it into the break to overflowing. The putty is thick and won't run so there's no need to prop the canoe or build a tape well.
3. When the putty is firm (about five minutes), slice off the excess with your pocketknife. Allow the remainder to cure completely (another ten minutes), then sand it level with progressive grits of sandpaper. Finish to silky smoothness with 400 grit wet sandpaper.
4. Spray paint the patch. When the paint has dried, blend the paint to match the hull with a mixture of paste wax and pumice. Or, polish with commercial fiberglass boat wax, which contains pumice.

The repair is hardly noticeable, and down time on the boat is less than an hour.

ABS Royalex hulls are so tough that they are nearly puncture proof. Repairs are usually made with fiberglass cloth and epoxy resin. Kits are available from nearly every company who manufactures these canoes.

If you own a fine wood-canvas canoe, you are probably well aware of how to maintain it. Old Town Canoe Company offers everything you need to restore these craft. Wood-canvas canoes never die; they just accumulate new parts. For detailed instructions on how to repair wood-canvas canoes, consult the American Red Cross's canoeing manual, which provides a wealth of information on the subject.

CHAPTER NINE

The Art of Car-Topping

Given enough rope—and time—anyone can tie down a canoe so it won't blow off a car. The fun comes when you have several boats to haul or when the wind whips to impressive speeds. Then you'd better know what you're doing or you may have an airborne missile on your hands!

The safest arrangement is to get a car-top carrier that bolts directly to the automobile's drip eaves—an insurmountable problem now that nearly all vehicles come with airplane-style doors. Fortunately, several companies offer fitted brackets for gutterless cars, and these have proven reliable over the long haul.

Even if you never plan to buy a second canoe, you will often need to shuttle a friend's, so be sure to order double-length (78 to 82 inches) racks—the factory-standard 48-inch carrier is not long enough to carry two canoes.

As an added precaution, canoes carried in pairs should have a boat cushion or piece of carpeting placed between them and tied to one of the canoes. It is also essential to secure carpeting or heater hose to crossbars so the rails won't be damaged. Many canoeists (myself included) simply won't allow their canoes to be carried on nonpadded racks!

FOR SAFETY'S SAKE, TIE 'EM DOWN

Most canoeists give only casual thought to securing their canoes to car-top carriers. A properly tied down canoe should show little, if any, movement, even in high winds at speeds well in excess of those legally posted. As a rule of thumb, each canoe carried should be tied down separately. This will eliminate many embarrassing problems at highway speeds.

Attach a stout ¼-inch nylon rope to each car rack. Run the lines over the belly of the canoe and secure them to the other side of the rack. Tie each as close as possible to the gunwales of the canoe to prevent wind-shift. The power-cinch (see chapter 10, Tying It All Together) is the most suitable knot and is the only one that should be used for tying down canoes. Additionally, tie two ropes to each end of the canoe and attach the free ends of these lines to their respective bumpers, as far apart as possible. Again, use a power-cinch. Make up a special set of nylon ropes with S-hooks at each end, or install steel eye-bolts in the bumpers. It is very difficult to attach naked ropes to bumpers properly. The sharp bumper edges can easily cut thick rope on a long auto trip if sufficient friction is generated by high winds. **Caution:** Avoid the use of rubber truck tie-downs. They have too much stretch and can cause problems if the canoe is buffeted by wind. Lastly, if you car-top two canoes on one car, use a separate belly rope for each canoe. This is in keeping with the aforementioned rule of thumb, and it will also help keep paired canoes from rubbing.

HOW DO YOU CARRY THREE CANOES ON A CAR RACK BUILT FOR TWO?

To carry a third canoe on a two car rack, mount two boats on the carriers as described, then place two 5-foot-long carpeted one-by-twos across the belly of each canoe. Center the third craft on top of these wooden supports and tie it to the metal crossbars and car bumpers. On a long trip it's a good idea to tie the ends of the one-by-twos to the steel carriers.

Canoe clubs frequently trek to the river with a half dozen or more canoes and kayaks piled high on a vehicle. (I think the record—established at a national whitewater event—is ten boats!) Such displays of civil engineering are impressive, but not necessarily safe. Most canoeists would agree that you're tempting fate whenever you carry more than three boats at a time on the overhead racks of a car. If you need to haul more than three canoes, use a trailer—it's much safer.

TRAILERING

The best way to carry large numbers of canoes is aboard a trailer built especially for the purpose. Be sure the trailer has good-size fenders so it won't throw dirt and gravel into the canoes and a high enough "tree" so the ends of the bottom canoes won't bottom-out on rutted roads. As always, use good nylon line, not rubber ropes, to secure the canoes to the trailer.

Caution: Well-tied-down canoes stiffen a trailer tree considerably. However, when the canoes are removed and the trailer is run empty over rough roads, substantial strain is placed on the unsupported tree. After a few years (or less!) of bouncing around, the crossbars usually give way and require rewelding. A number of methods have been used to stiffen the crossbars, but the best is a vertical strut (see figure 9-1) which spans two bars. The strut bolts in place with wing-nuts and swings aside to load and unload the canoes. This setup virtually eliminates stress...and trailer breakdown.

PROCEDURES FOR CARRYING FRAGILE CANOES

Ultralight fiberglass, Kevlar, and wood-strip canoes should be handled with a loving touch. They should be carried on padded crossbars or foam gunwale pads only and tied with clean, large-diameter (¼- to ⅜-inch) ropes, which won't gall their delicate skin.

You can break the spine of a lightweight canoe if you snug its ends too tightly, so it's preferable to tie *only* the bow to the front bumper. If you cinch down the tail, you may bow the hull and damage it.

If you're hauling two canoes on a double rack, place the fragile canoe on the right side (passenger side) of the carriers. This will allow the sturdier (and more rigidly tied) craft on the driver's side to take the abuse of high winds generated by passing trucks. If you car-top three canoes, put the most fragile one on top.

SPECIAL CONSIDERATIONS WHEN TRAVELING IN VERY HIGH WINDS

In very high winds you may want to rig a bridle around the bow (windshield end) of your car-topped canoe. To make the bridle, tie a length of rope tightly around the hull near the seat (loop it through the seat supports) and secure it to the

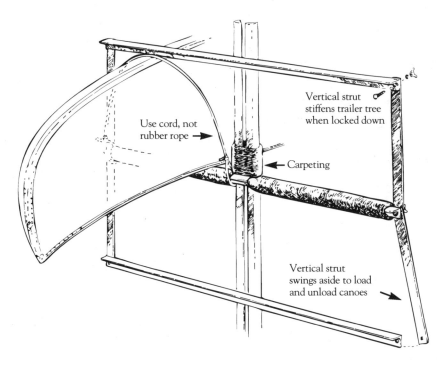

Use cord, not rubber rope →

Vertical strut stiffens trailer tree when locked down

← Carpeting

Vertical strut swings aside to load and unload canoes →

Figure 9-1 Stiffen the tree of your canoe trailer by adding removable vertical struts. This brace will take the strain off the cross bars when the empty trailer is shuttled.

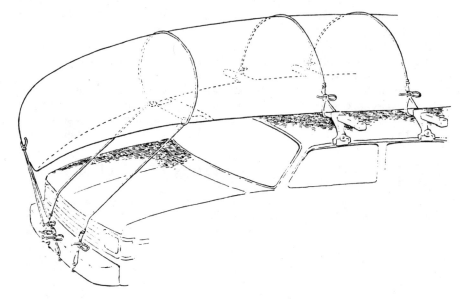

Figure 9-2 In very high winds you may want to rig a bridle around the bow of your canoe. All lines should go through eye-bolts or S-hooks on the bumper.

bumper (figure 9-2). The bridle will absorb wind stress and take the load off brass and plastic fittings, which may break or bend under stress.

PART THREE

Applied Skills

Tying it all Together

You can get along very nicely with just the sheet bend and power-cinch. Add the double half-hitch and bowline, and you'll be set for every emergency.

THE DOUBLE HALF-HITCH (TWO-HALF-HITCHES)
The double half-hitch is useful for tying a rope to a tree or to the towing link of a canoe. The knot is very secure and tends to tighten itself when a load is applied to the rope.

Figure 10-1 Double Half-Hitch

THE SHEET BEND

Use the sheet bend for tying two ropes together. The knot works well even if the rope sizes differ greatly. The sheet bend is about the only knot that can be effectively used to join the ends of slippery polypropylene rope.

It is important that the free ends of the sheet bend be on the same side, as shown in figure 10-2. The knot will work if the ends are on opposite sides, but will be less reliable.

Figure10-2 Sheet Bend

THE BOWLINE

The bowline is a very secure knot which won't slip—regardless of the load applied. It is commonly used by mountain climbers to tie their climbing ropes around their waists. Use this knot whenever you want to put a nonslip loop on the end of a line.

Beginners are often told to make the bowline by forming a loop, or "rabbit hole." The rabbit (free end of the rope) comes up through the hole, around the tree (opposite or long end of the rope shown in figure 10-3) and back down the hole. The bowline will slip a few inches before it tightens, so allow an extra-long free end.

Figure10-3 The Bowline

THE POWER-CINCH

Perhaps the most ingenious hitch to come along in recent years is the power-cinch (there seems to be no widely accepted name for this hitch, so I took the liberty of naming it the power-cinch), which effectively replaces the tautline hitch and functions as a powerful pulley when used properly. Skilled canoeists use this pulley knot almost exclusively for tying canoes on cars. It is also widely used by truckers who tie heavy loads in place. The power-cinch may be the canoeist's most useful hitch.

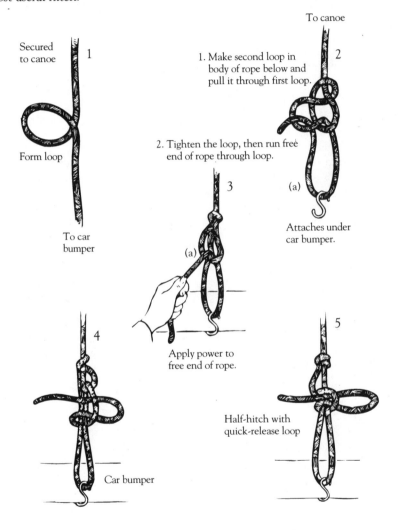

Secured to canoe

1

Form loop

To car bumper

To canoe

1. Make second loop in body of rope below and pull it through first loop.

2

2. Tighten the loop, then run free end of rope through loop.

3

(a)

(a)

Attaches under car bumper.

Apply power to free end of rope.

4

Car bumper

5

Half-hitch with quick-release loop

Figure 10-4 Power Cinch

Begin the power-cinch by forming the loop shown in figure 10-4 step 1. Pull the loop through as in step 2. It is important that the loop be formed *exactly* as shown. The loop will look okay if you make it backwards, but it won't work.

If the loop is formed as in step 2, a simple tug on the rope will eliminate it. This is preferable to the common practice of tying a knot in the loop, which, after being exposed to a load, is almost impossible to get out.

If you are tying a canoe into place on top of a car, tie one end of the rope to the canoe's bow or stern and snap the steel hook on the other end of the rope to the car's bumper. Run the free end of the rope (a) through the loop in step 2. Now apply power to the free end. You have, in effect, created a pulley with a two-to-one mechanical advantage.

Complete the hitch by securing a double half hitch around the body of the rope or use a quick-release loop as illustrated.

THE QUICK-RELEASE LOOP

There's nothing more frustrating than untying a bunch of tight knots when you're breaking camp in the morning. If you end your knots with a quick-release loop like that illustrated in figure 10-4, step 5, you'll be able to untie your ties with a single pull. Form the quick-release feature by running the free end of the rope back through the completed knot—same as making a bow when you tie your shoes.

Use a simple overhand knot with a quick-release loop to seal the stuff sacks that contain your sleeping bag and personal gear. The plastic "cord-locks" sold for this purpose are for people who don't know how to tie effective quick-release knots.

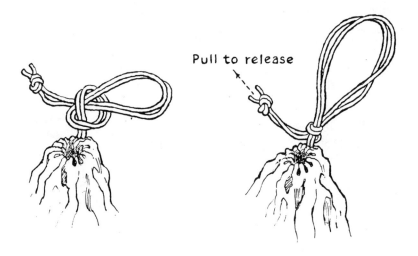

Pull to release

Figure 10-5 Secure your stuff sacks with a quick-release loop.

SECURING A LINE

On a wilderness trip several years ago one canoe of our party swamped in a heavy rapid. There was a bouldery falls about 200 yards downstream, and it was imperative that we get a rope to the wet canoeists immediately in order to avoid disaster. Luckily, a 50-foot line was at hand and was properly coiled for throwing. The line was heaved to the two men who were hanging on to the gunwales of the water-filled canoe. Fortunately, the men caught the rope, and both they and the canoe were pulled safely to shore, avoiding what might have been a serious mishap.

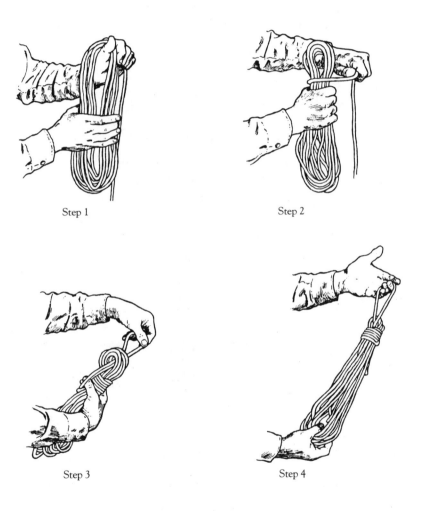

Step 1

Step 2

Step 3

Step 4

Figure 10-6 Securing a Line: Steps 1–4

You should always keep your ropes coiled and ready for use. The best system I have found is an old Navy method:

1. Coil the rope (taking care to lay each coil carefully into place), grasp the main body of it with one hand and place your thumb through the eye of the coils to hold them in place, as shown in figure 10-6, step 1.
2. Remove the last two coils of rope, take this long free end and wind it around the main body of the rope several times (figure 10-6, step 2). Wind the free end downward, toward the hand holding the rope body. Wind evenly and snugly. Don't make the coils too tight.
3. Form a loop with the free end of the rope, as shown in step 3, and push it through the eye of the rope body.

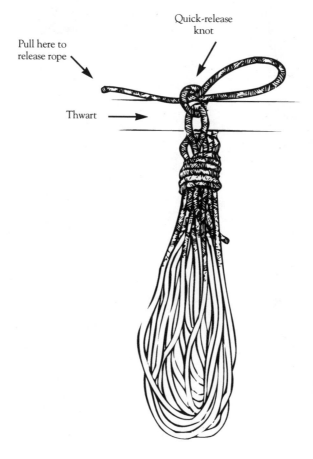

Quick-release
knot

Pull here to
release rope

Thwart

Figure 10-7 Bind your 50-foot line by the old Navy method outlined in figure 10-6 then tie it to a thwart as illustrated here. A quick pull of the "free end" releases the rope instantly.

CANOEING AND CAMPING

4. Grasp the wound coils with one hand and the rope body with the other hand and slide the coils upward tightly against the loop. The rope is now coiled and secured (step 4). Pulling the front end of the rope will release the line, which can quickly be made ready for throwing.

I bind all my 50-foot utility ropes in this manner and store them under a packflap so they'll be quickly available when I need them. When running whitewater, I often keep a throwing line tied around a thwart as illustrated in figure 10-7. A single pull releases the line from the thwart; a second tug makes it ready for use. Fast and convenient...and possibly a life-saver!

CHAPTER ELEVEN

Solo Canoeing is Different

Sunrise on any river, U.S.A. A damp morning mist, warmed by the day's beginning, rises reluctantly above the cool, green water. Beneath the slowly burning fog an ever-growing ribbon of gold expands confidently across the horizon.

In awesome silence you slip your trim, light solo canoe into the awaiting riffles, while, nearby, friends in a tandem canoe follow suit. A gentle push of the paddle sets you free and in harmony with the determined current.

For a while you paddle powerfully, each stroke crisp and well timed. The quick canoe responds eagerly and glides whisper quiet at what seems to be incredible speed. Around a bend a great blue heron curiously looks your way. In awkward slow motion he stretches his wings and with casual assuredness begins to fly. The muffled hiss of your wake has broken the spell!

The sun is in full posture now and the day is flooded with its warmth and light. Everywhere the sights and sounds of the river entice you to linger, so you rest your paddle, laze back, and wait for your friends to catch up. Above, puffy clouds of hushed white whisk quietly by, and for a time you are left alone with your dreams and the delights of the river.

Then you hear it—the hollow drone of rushing water. Falls? The shock of realization brings you bolt upright. Your eyes search knowingly for the danger signs—a broken tree line or crest of dancing white. Then you see it—a narrow band of discontinuous water that stretches entirely across your path.

Ledge! You call loudly to your friends behind. But don't panic; you're in control. A few well-placed backstrokes bring the little canoe swiftly to shore.

The falls, a sheer 6-foot drop over sharp granite, is not negotiable. And neither are the rapids below. You'll have to take the half mile portage that's indicated on your map. Singlehandedly, you shoulder your thirty-five-pound canoe while a few yards away your friends struggle with their tandem craft of twice the weight. A smug smile flashes briefly as you jubilantly strike off down the trail. You're beginning to discover the joys of the solo canoe!

Part way through the portage you ascend a long, steep hill, at the top of which stands a well-worn canoe rest. But the little boat is no burden, so you unhesitatingly continue on. Seconds later you hear the hollow clunk of a canoe being set on the wooden brace you just passed—a reminder that your tandem friends don't share your unencumbered feeling. The smile returns!

Now the trail descends quickly and you move along at a furious pace. A glint of white suddenly appears among the blanketing foliage and you know the river is near.

You set the little canoe at the water's edge and stare unbelievingly at the river. You've canoed in low water before, but this is ridiculous! A shallow rock fan stretches well into the next bend, perhaps a quarter mile. There are 3, maybe 4, inches of water lying between the water's surface and its pebble bottom. And everywhere huge round rocks protrude like polished marbles on an earthen field. No way can the big canoe get through there without grinding, scraping, breaking.

But you can!

As you gingerly board your solo canoe for the slalom run, you watch amusedly as your friends put on their wading shoes. "It's gonna be along walk." you tease. "Sure glad I can ride!"

Once under way, the little canoe comes alive. It leans when you lean, goes forward, backward, sideways on command. There's no argument from a partner, your spouse, or your mother-in-law. A screwup is a screwup, and you have no one to blame but yourself.

You discover that the tightest turns are possible if you brace far out on your paddle and lean the canoe until its gunwale barely touches the water. Ahead, are a cluster of rocks with a 2-foot channel between. No problem; you tilt the canoe to one side and scoot cleanly through.

Now you're both bow and stern—sweeping, drawing, prying, bracing. Occasionally the muffled screech of fiberglass impacting rock rewards your indecision and carelessness. But no matter; these surface scratches do much more harm to your ego than your canoe.

Within minutes it's over, and you find yourself drifting aimlessly in the deep, still water below the rapid. A few lazy backstrokes bring you to shore, where you get out and stretch...and wait for your friends to finish lining their canoe through the rock garden you just paddled!

These, then, are the joys of the solo canoe—joys that become more intense as the years creep by and you suddenly discover that you're not as athletic as you used to be. Small-framed men and women need no introduction to the pleasures of soloing, for they more than anyone else "understand" what it means to be always last on the portage trail and forever chained to the bow seat of a tandem canoe. Tough day at the office? Perhaps an hour's play on a park pond will provide the relaxation you need. Got a canoe trip planned and can't find a partner? Great; take your solo canoe! Extended wilderness tripping? You bet! A well-designed

Figure 11-1 Got a trip planned and can't find a partner? Great, take your solo canoe! Unless you plan to bring along the kitchen sink, you'll have more space than you can possibly use.
Photo credit: Sawyer Canoe Company

"little boat" can carry at least three hundred pounds—nearly half the weight of an average tandem canoe. Unless you plan to bring along the kitchen sink, you'll have more space than you can possibly use.

"But I'm a family person," you say. "How can I take the kids along if I paddle alone?" Well, you can't, of course. But wouldn't it be nice if the children could paddle *their own* canoe rather than ride in yours? Easy enough if you outfit your solo canoe with seats fore and aft. Now, your teenie-boppers can experience the joy of canoeing in a boat that's suited to their dimensions. Meanwhile, the grownups can tag along behind in a big canoe. Two canoes—one tandem, one solo—per family is not an extravagance; it's common sense...and a delightfully good time!

White water, flat water, local streams, or the deep wilderness. The solo canoe will go anywhere a tandem canoe will go—a bit more slowly perhaps, but with a grace, style, and elegance that is unmatched by the most sophisticated large canoe.

Solo canoes *are* different, and many of the procedures and equipment used to paddle and portage them also are different.

EQUIPMENT

Paddles

You must have two paddles in the event one breaks. Paddle length is determined by the reach of your arms and the style boat you paddle (see chapter 5 for specifics). Flatwater racing canoes require short paddles—50 to 53 inches long, preferably with angled blades. Whitewater slalom and traditionally styled touring canoes are more compatible with longer paddles—54 to 60 inches.

Some canoeists prefer to use a double paddle for some or all of their paddling. A well designed solo canoe will dance across the water when powered by twin blades; however, the standard kayak paddle is too short; you need a length of 81/2 or 9 feet (not commonly available), which means you'll have to make your own. Be sure the paddle breaks apart at the center for storage between uses.

Double paddles are considered "gauche" in fashionable canoeing circle. To many (myself included), soloing is an art form—one that necessarily demands efficient use of the single blade. Nonetheless, don't let me or anyone else spoil your pleasure. Double paddles are efficient. If you like them, use them!

Portage Yoke

The yoke *must* be removable (unlike those used on tandem canoes) so it won't interfere with paddling (you sit or kneel in the middle of the canoe, remember?) The best arrangement is to attach the yoke to the gunwales with hardwood clamps and wingnuts or buy a pair of indestructible aluminum yoke brackets from Old Town or Mad River Canoe companies.

Knee Pads

The advantage of solo canoes over kayaks is versatility. You can sit or kneel (or even stand) if you wish. In rough water kneeling is an "option" in big, steady tandem canoes; in "tender" solo canoes it is an absolute must! Glue knee pads into the bottom of your canoe for the ultimate comfort.

Packs

For day trips a small nylon pack is fine, as long as it's not too heavy. A solo canoe is sensitive to proper trim (the difference between the draft at each end). A few misplaced pounds, fore or aft of dead center, may unbalance it and adversely affect performance. Consequently, it's unwise to place "all of your eggs in one basket," even if they all will fit. It's better to use two packs—a large soft (no frame) tripping pack of some sort and a medium sized day pack.

I place food, sleeping gear, tent and cooking items into the large pack and set it in front of my feet. The small pack, which contains extra clothes, rain gear, sweater, and other frequently used essentials, goes behind the seat (some canoeists reverse the position of these packs). By moving the packs forward or back, I can balance the canoe perfectly.

An annoying characteristic of all open solo canoes is that they are always wet inside. Every time you change sides with your paddle ("HUT"), which you do often to steer and rest muscles, water drips off the blade and into the canoe. Keep a large sponge secured beneath a loop of shock cord tied around the side of your seat frame. Sponging out accumulated water is a never-ending process!

For a week-long trip your solo canoe will easily carry more cargo than you'll ever want to bring along. Nevertheless, that's no excuse to bring too much. The price of gluttony is a sluggish canoe, or at best an unspirited one. If you choose items carefully, your heaviest pack should weigh less than fifty pounds and your light pack around fifteen pounds. (See chapter 3 for a discussion of the things you really need.) Carry the heavy pack, paddles, life vest, and camera over the portage first. On the second trip take the canoe and small day pack. This works out to about fifty-five pounds per trip.

Touring the wilds in a solo canoe is easier if you travel in the company of other canoes since you can share the weight of community essentials—tent, cook set, axe, saw, and so forth. I recently completed a ten-day canoe trip on an Ontario river along with three other solo friends. My share of the outfit (including food and personal gear) was sixty pounds—less than I commonly carry on tandem canoe trips of the same length.

It's important to fit all your camping gear into two packs so you can complete the portages in three trips (one round trip plus the return leg.) A third pack means *two* additional portage crossings, so plan wisely and "go light."

Map and Compass

You are your own partner in a solo canoe; there's no time to fumble for navigational aids when you're fighting waves on a wind-tossed lake. A few moments of distraction and you may find yourself lost...or upside down!

For these reasons it's essential to secure your map under a loop of shockcord strung through holes drilled in the front thwart, as suggested in chapter 2. Also, I carry two compasses—a small but highly accurate Silva Huntsman (for plotting the course from the map) and a Silva wrist model (for easy reference while paddling). The Huntsman rests in my shirt pocket, protected against loss by a lanyard attached to a buttonhole. I keep the wrist compass strapped to the forward thwart. With this setup my map and compass are always visible, regardless of how actively I paddle.

PADDLING ALONE

There is but one seat in a solo canoe so you have little option of where to sit. The lone paddler must have complete control over both ends of the canoe, possible only when he or she is seated near the center.

If you don't own a solo canoe, it is possible to paddle a big canoe alone. However, you must assume a position just aft of center by rigging up some sort of kneeling thwart or seat here. Many people prefer to paddle a tandem canoe alone from the stern seat because the canoe is so narrow at this point. But this practice is extremely dangerous since it knocks the canoe way out of trim. The bow rides

Figure11-2 Solo canoes set you free to follow your star in your own way at your own pace.

high in the air while the stern sinks low. The effect is that of paddling a 7-foot canoe with a 10-foot overhang. The slightest breeze will capsize you instantly. Also, any degree of control or speed is impossible.

Some canoeists recommend that you solo a tandem canoe from the stern and weight the bow with logs or duffel. Again, a mistake. You can't control the bow of a canoe if you're located 15 feet away at the opposite end of the lever arm.

As you gain solo experience, you'll develop a repertoire of special strokes—the C, draw, low brace, and so forth. But you don't need all these to use and enjoy your solo canoe. In fact, the most efficient way to paddle alone is to simply switch sides whenever the boat begins to waver off course. Though some people consider the practice boring, it is very powerful and state of the art for racing.

Some paddlers prefer a hybrid style of paddling. They use a doublepaddle on open water and change to a short single blade and racing-switch-stroke on the river. In rapids they select a long single paddle and twist their way between obstacles with a variety of hard-to-define sophisticated strokes. That's the beauty of soloing: You're free to chase your star in your own way at your own pace.

You'll find a wealth of solo procedures and paddling techniques in my book *Basic Essentials of Solo Canoeing* (ICS Books, 1991).

CANOEING AND CAMPING

CHAPTER TWELVE

Day-Tripping

IT PAYS TO BE PREPARED
BUT DON'T GO OVERBOARD

D ay tripping—where all the hours of planning, packing, and "fear of rain" come together. You're at the river at last, sun rising warmly to the newborn day, and there's not a cloud in the sky anywhere.

You rest momentarily against the car fender and watch your friends repeat the age-old procedures for "putting in." Down the way an older man and woman struggle to remove an aluminum canoe from the high roof of their van. You leap to their assistance.

It's a bit of a hike from the roadway to the mud bank of the river, so you offer to portage the canoe the entire way. On your return you're greeted by gentle smiles and gracious thanks. What a way to begin the day!

With the help of your spouse you unload your canoe and carry it down the bank to the waiting river. There's no "landing" per se, just a small, sandy flat that is already occupied by a half-dozen canoes. "Dang!" you mutter. "No place for me." Unwillingly, you set down the canoe on the steep incline—bow in the river, stern on land. For safety's sake you tie the stern painter to a nearby tree. A smug smile flashes briefly when you discover that no one but you remembered to attach ropes to the ends of his canoe. Ah...expertise!

Your eyes knowingly inventory each item. In the big packsack is a change of clothes, light jacket, and rain gear for everyone, along with two pairs of socks (just in case!) for six-year-old Peggy Anne. And it's all safely protected from rain and the river by two nested plastic sacks.

Your inventory continues: two adult-size life jackets and a "pee wee" vest for little Peggy, a small ice chest, a closed cell foam pad for your daughter to sleep on, an aluminized space blanket for the picnic shore lunch, and a nylon pack filled with fried chicken and chips, candy bars, paper plates and cups, silverware, and paper towels for cleanup. And, oh yes, toilet paper in a Ziploc bag.

Tied to the packstrap is a sturdy nylon bag for hauling out trash—yours and others who are less thoughtful!

It's quite a heap, but you may need it all. At any rate, it pays to be prepared.

Two trips down the bank and everything is safely stowed inside the waiting canoe. This will be a simple float trip—no real rapids—so there's no reason to tie anything in. Now all that's left is to wait until the cars return from the "takeout" point. Within the hour you'll be on your way.

The shuttle is completed and the apparent disorder of earlier comes to an abrupt halt. Suddenly everyone knows exactly what they're doing. In a flash canoes are loaded and launched. The day begins!

The first few minutes you paddle hard. It feels good to stretch your muscles, to work out the city kinks. Then, as the uniqueness of the day begins to fade, your strokes slow to an easy all-day pace.

Around the bend you spot a dappled fawn standing ankle-deep in water near the shore. A hush falls on the group and someone points. In unison everyone rests their paddle and simply watches the deer.

Downstream the river changes from stagnant backwater to joyful riffles. Peggy tries her miniature paddle and drops it instantly. No matter; it trails safely behind, tethered to a length of cord you attached for just such an occasion.

A dozen bends later you come upon the quiet pool that marks trip's end. Already there's a jam-up at the landing, so you rest your paddle and just wait around. Another canoe pulls alongside and you strike up a friendly conversation. You've never met these folks before, but immediately there's a bond. As you bid farewell, you both agree to meet again on next week's day trip.

These, then, are the joys of the river. Joys born of love and friendship, of artistry and motion. The river passes as a fleeting moment: but it is always there, waiting for you to return again.

CHECK LIST OF EQUIPMENT FOR DAY TRIPPING

Besides the obvious—life jackets and paddles—you'll need:

- Complete change of clothes for everyone (in a waterproof pack)
- Light jacket or sweater
- Brimmed hat and sunglasses
- Rain gear
- First-aid kit
- Pocketknife
- Matches
- Ropes (lines) for the ends of your canoe
- Water bottle, soft drinks, snacks, and so forth.
- Flashlight: It's amazing how many trips begin in daylight and end in darkness.
- Map of route and compass.

CHAPTER THIRTEEN

Tripping with Tots and Teens

TRIPPING WITH TOTS

The Indians call it "chautauqua," which means "traveling show," and it aptly describes a family of canoeists on a pleasant float downstream. Put these together in the same canoe: Mom and Dad, a wiggling two year old and inquisitive five year old, waterproof packsacks filled with dry clothes, an ice chest stocked with pop, a Thermos of milk, bags of disposable diapers, sunscreen and bug dope, toilet paper, facial tissues and Handi-Wipes, jackets, hats, paddles, a camera and pair of stuffed teddy bears, potato chips, pretzels, and candy snacks...and the view from dockside is in every sense, a "chautauqua!"

At these times you're sure to wonder if all the pretrip planning and packing, the stern instructions to the kids, and the hopeful prayers for a brilliant rain-free day are really worth the joys of a family canoe outing. Is canoeing with children all that it's cracked up to be? Or is it really more trouble than it's worth?

The first time you see the bright eyes of your child come alive with wonder at the sight of a big blue heron standing knee-deep in sea-green duckweed a dozen feet away or soothe the frightened cry that results when a foot-long fish jumps brashly across your bow or thrill to the bubbly laughter of a breezy glide down gentle rapids, you'll "know." Then no amount of pre- or post trip drudgery will ever again chain you to the dull confines of house or garden work when on the river there awaits the sunlit morning of a new day.

Children are magic. And canoes are the perfect vehicle to transport them into the ever-changing, always entertaining world of nature. There's no better way to keep a youthful heart than to paddle with young people. Canoes provide all the entertainment kids need to provide all the laughs you need!

So much for philosophy. Now let's be deadly honest: Canoeing with children can be a trying experience, even when you do everything right. Your role as parent and leader requires canoe-handling knowledge, a perceptive eye, and patience, patience, patience! Even then, don't expect miracles. Kids *will* behave like kids.

THE RIGHT ATTITUDE

Uppermost in your mind should be the realization that you're canoeing for the *sake of the children*, not the adults. Everything should be structured around their safety, well-being, and concerns. I've seen parents set toddlers on the cold, damp floor of a metal canoe without so much as a square of plastic for insulation. Without a dry place to sit, a comfortable backrest, and a soft pad to sleep on, they'll respond by crying, screaming, and kicking—exactly what you can't tolerate in the tippy confines of a canoe. The right equipment and a detailed battle plan will eliminate most problems.

FIRST, GET SOME INSTRUCTION!

The greatest safety margin that you can provide for your children is for you to be both a competent swimmer and a reasonably good canoeist. These two factors will keep you out of trouble in almost all situations in which you have nonswimmers aboard. If there is a canoe club nearby, join it. If not, read and reread the good books on canoeing available in your local library. Then, get out and practice— without kids. At any rate, do join your state canoe association. As a member of a canoe club, you will become acquainted with other canoeing families, and your mind will be more at ease knowing there are others to share your experiences and to help with problems.

THE PROPER EQUIPMENT

First and foremost is the life jacket. Toddlers absolutely must wear their life jackets at all times. A bit of psychology helps—and generally this means that both mom and dad set an example. Since the rocking motion of a canoe is conducive to extra-long naps, it is important that the life jackets your children wear be extremely comfortable ones that they can sleep in.

Several companies now make specialized life jackets for preschoolers, all of which have been thoroughly tested and Coast Guard approved. Although expensive, they are an excellent investment for the safety of your child, since children will wear them contentedly even through their naps. Swim aids, while more attractive and less expensive than Coast Guard-approved life jackets, should be avoided, for they will not keep the head of a nonswimmer afloat.

The bottom of a canoe (aluminum models, at least) may run only a few degrees warmer than the temperature of the water. Consequently, it is important to cover the bottom with adequate cushioning for both insulation and comfort. The best solution is to place an air mattress, nylon-covered foam pad, or piece of Ensolite foam on the bottom of the canoe for the children to sit on and later to curl up on for a nap. Children will want to sit up and view the countryside, so a backrest of some kind should be provided. A foam cushion makes a suitable backrest when propped up against a canoe thwart, and when nap time rolls around, it makes a good pillow as well.

Each child should have his or her favorite blanket and toy. By all means, provide a canoe paddle of miniature dimensions, for children love to paddle (it is wise to tie a string to the paddle and to secure this string to a canoe thwart). Don't become disenchanted by your passenger's inability to paddle properly. Let kids play with their paddles as they wish (just so they don't hit each other or you), for this is part of their good time.

A complete change of clothes from nose to toes must be provided, and rain gear is very important. The best rain covering for toddlers is a poncho. The hood and extra-long body of the poncho will cover a child completely. A less-expensive solution is to provide each child with a plastic leaf-and-lawn-sized garbage bag. Merely cut a slit for the head in the top of the bag and furnish a "sou'wester" style hat to go with it.

It is also advisable to bring along a spare blanket. When children fall asleep in the canoe, they may need additional insulation not provided by their security blankets. Lastly, a lightweight nylon or plastic fly of about 8 feet by 10 feet is desirable for shelter in case you want to get off the water during a heavy rain or as a cover for the kids when they are sleeping, should a light rain begin.

Proper footgear is always a concern. After years of canoeing with children I'm completely won over to sneakers and galoshes (or slip-on rubber boots). This combination keeps feet dry in rain and when wading ashore or exploring the river's edge. Once aboard the canoe—or in camp—the boots are quickly removable.

In addition to food and drink for the day, bring a Thermos of milk for the kids and some penny candy. Plan to stop for a few minutes each hour, and allow time for fun and games during the lunch break. Generally, river trips of about ten miles are ideal; longer trips tend to get somewhat trying for both children and adults, and three or four hours on the water is plenty with young children. For toddlers in diapers, the disposable kind are indispensable. Take several, packed in a waterproof plastic bag, and place used diapers in a plastic bag to be brought home for proper disposal.

Insects: Nothing can spoil a trip faster than determined mosquitoes and black flies. Repellents are essential but mustn't be too strong. Super-effective products that contain more than 40 percent DEET (diethylmeta-toluamide) may be too caustic for sensitive young skin. Citronella or cream-base formulas are best. If bugs are really a problem, provide a headnet and gloves for everyone.

It should go without saying that river sections with rapids should be avoided—even by highly skilled canoeists. Very mild, bouncing water can, of course, be paddled and adds to the fun. A final word of safety: If you have two nonswimmers aboard, decide before the trip how you will handle an upset should it occur. Generally one parent goes after each child. *Do not* take three nonswimmers on a canoe trip when there are only two swimmers to watch them. Should you overturn, your first responsibility is to your children. With everyone wearing life jackets in a slow-moving river or placid lake, rescue should present no problems, especially if another canoe is nearby.

TRIPPING WITH TEENS

Scenario: the youth director of your church just phoned to ask if you the local canoeing and camping expert—would help him lead some teenagers on a week-long canoe trip to "Any Park, U.S.A."

Flattered by his confidence in your ability, you dutifully answer, "Sure." After all, you'd planned to canoe the park this summer anyway. Why not share the experience with a group of appreciative kids and, in the process, teach this inexperienced youth leader the ropes?

"Uh, how many kids are we talking about?" you ask.

"I dunno, maybe eighteen if all the older kids go," he answers.

"Eighteen fourteen year olds, and just you and me? You've got to be kidding!"

"Hey, I took twelve of 'em to Mexico alone last year. No problem. This time there'll be two of us. You handle the canoeing and camping stuff; I'll take care of the rest. Okay?"

Numbly, you mumble acceptance, keenly aware that the "canoeing and camping" stuff says it all. Your spouse lovingly pats your shoulder and offers to help. "Congratulations, Honey, you're the leader!"

GETTING STARTED

Make no mistake, *you*, not the tenderfoot youth director, are the leader, and you'd best make this fact abundantly clear at the start. *You* must have the final say in matters of organization, safety, equipment, training, routes, and rules of the road. Even the menu must reflect your knowledge of backcountry needs and what kids will eat. The counselor may make recommendations, of course, but it is *your* responsibility to bring these kids back with a smile on their face and a song in their heart. Call this guy back right now and set the record straight. You should take the job only after agreement is reached here.

MEETING THE KIDS

The first order of business is to meet the kids and parents, show some slides and canoeing gear to gather interest, explain expectations, and go over the necessary forms. Each participant must have a copy of the following documents:

Parent Medical Release: If a youngster is injured and must be evacuated to a hospital, the medical release gives the attending physician authority to administer drugs or perform surgery without the okay of a parent. A simple statement that gives you the authority to act in lieu of a parent in the event of emergency is all you need. Include the phone number of parent(s) or guardian(s), family physician, and a relative or friend who can be reached in an emergency. You *must* carry this document on the canoe trip.

Parent Permission Form: You cannot take kids across a state or international border without permission of a parent. This fact was made abundantly clear to me some years ago when I attempted to cross into Canada with nine teenagers in tow. When the young customs officer refused to admit us, the kids began to act like normal teenagers. They whined and cried and claimed that I was their dad. Then they began to yell and throw things. Finally, the poor woman could take no more and we were reluctantly waved on through. When we arrived in Thunder Bay, I bought them all pizza for their cunning bravery in the face of adversity.

Swim Form: Most summer camps have a 100-yard swim requirement. Frankly, I think that's overkill for a gentle river or lake-country canoe trip. If a youngster can swim 50 feet unaided and is comfortable in deep water while wearing a life jacket, that's enough. Conversely, it's unwise to take along nonswimmers, no matter how loudly they or their parents complain.

Behavioral Contract: Cigarettes, alcohol, or hard drugs can ruin a trip in short order. Teenagers *must* understand that they will be immediately dropped from the trip if they're caught with any illegal substance. Don't minimize the importance of the behavioral contract. It is your ticket to a sane, well-mannered good time!

Equipment List: I require that teenagers religiously follow the equipment list detailed in Appendix 1. I go over each item, carefully explaining the rationale for every choice. Kids and parents will want to save money by substituting plastic ponchos for reliable two-piece nylon rain suits, tennis shoes for sturdy boots, hooded cotton sweatshirts for wool or pile sweaters, cheap slumber bags for genuine sleeping bags, and blue jeans for quick-drying cotton/polyester pants.

Allow no substitutes! You are the responsible adult on this trip. Everyone in your charge must be prepared to endure a week of cold, penetrating rain and muddy portages without complaint. That means wool, pile, polypropylene, or acrylic clothing, sturdy boots, and rain gear that won't destruct on the first portage.

Youngsters can find what they need at surplus stores and garage sales. In their search for the "right" stuff, it pays to remind them that a canoe trip is not a fashion show. What looks good and what works are often two different matters!

GROUP SIZE

Five teenagers per adult leader is about right. Nine is the absolute maximum! Split up groups larger than ten (including the leader). Large groups are noisy and wreak havoc on the environment—the reasons why most U.S. and Canadian wilderness areas impose a maximum limit on party size. Remember this if you have to split the group: Strive for a fifty-fifty gender split, and pair everyone with at least one good friend.

Question: John, Tom, and Bill are close friends. Alone, they are well-mannered, good kids. But put them together and all hell breaks loose. Since there are only two groups on this canoe trip, you can remove only one of them from the trio. You should (a) give all three their money back and tell them they can't go, (b) put all three together and take your chances, or (c) put one of the three in a separate group.

Answer: B and C are both reasonable choices. I've found that kids who cause trouble back home are often wonderful in the outdoors. In fact, some of my best teenage crews have been comprised of "at risk" kids who go the extra mile to impress their friends and me. The wilderness is foreign turf to most teenagers, and respect is earned by doing more than your fair share in camp and on the portages. Keep an open mind—you might be pleasantly surprised!

GROUP GEAR

If you want to really evaluate a piece of equipment, give it to a teenager for a week. Kids have an uncanny way of damaging or losing whatever they touch. On one of my trips a boy burned up a new boot and part of his sleeping bag. He also lost a wool shirt and life jacket. While fishing he cast out his lure with such force that the reel and rod tip flew into the lake! Sometime during the trip he broke an "unbreakable" synthetic paddle!

For this reason *do not* borrow canoes and gear from anyone whose friendship you want to retain. Renting is safer, especially if the kids know they will have to pay for damages. A twenty dollar damage deposit, to be reimbursed at trip's end, will make the point abundantly clear.

Remember these equipment tips: Fourteen-year-old boys and girls are perfectly capable of carrying seventy-five pound canoes—that is, if they have a properly fitted yoke. The pads on standard canoe yokes are spaced too wide for narrow teen shoulders. Yoke pads should be set 6½ to 7 inches apart (inside measurement) rather than the customary 7½ to 8½ inches.

Make downsized wood yokes for all your rental canoes and secure them to the gunwales with quickly removable wood or metal clamps. Most outfitters will allow you to remove their yokes and install your own if you supply the labor. When traveling with three to a canoe, remove the yoke to provide more room for your passenger.

OTHER ESSENTIALS

Scenario: The trip begins in light rain, which intensifies throughout the day. By the time you camp, it's coming down in cold, determined sheets. You have polypropylene and pile, a sophisticated watertight pack, and a class-act tent; the kids have cotton and acrylics, aging Duluth packs with patched plastic liners, well-abused rental tents, and no knowledge whatsoever as to how to keep things dry.

As the leader it's your job to keep hot meals coming and a dry roof over your crew. As a wilderness canoeist, you know what gear is necessary, you just need more of it. Be sure you carry these important items:

- One 4-mil-thick plastic groundcloth for the inside of every tent. Make each groundcloth oversize so it "flows" up the sidewalls of the tent. Water that wicks through worn fabric and floor seams will be trapped under the plastic and the tent will stay dry in heavy rain.
- One 10-foot-by-12-foot nylon rain tarp for every five people. Build a fire beneath and string a clothesline under the fly so the kids can dry wet gear.
- Two one-burner or one two-burner stoves per each group of ten.

- A sharp folding saw and hand axe. All wood is cut with the folding saw. The axe is used only as a splitting wedge; it is never used for chopping! I permit only one method of splitting (figures 13-1 and 13-2). The hand axe is set lightly into the upright log with just enough force to hold it in place. Then, the splitter grasps the through with a chunk of log. There are no "axidents" because the tool is never swung through the air!
- A 20- to 30-cup tea or coffee pot to satisfy the demand for soup and hot chocolate.
- Sitting pad: Most teen groups travel with three to a canoe, which means that one person rides "dead weight" in the cold, wet bottom of the hull. A sitting pad—boat cushion or square of waterproof foam—for each passenger is essential.

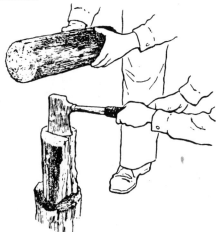

Figure 13-1 Splitting wood is easy if you use the axe as a splitting wedge rather than a "chopping" tool. Thick logs can easily be split by this method.

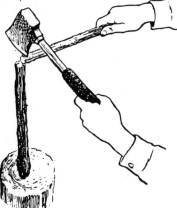

Figure 13-2 Kindling splits easier from the end grain—a process that is made easier (and safer!) if you use a stick of wood to hold the upright piece in place.

Accidents invariably fall into the following categories:

- Cuts due to whittling. Prevention? *Do not* allow kids to whittle!
- Blisters. Bring plenty of Spenco Second Skin.
- Sprained ankles (often results from horsing around). Worst sprain I ever saw resulted when a girl fell off the log on which she was dancing. It was midnight and she was showing her friends a new routine! Fortunately, I had an air splint and plenty of aspirin.
- Foreign object in the eye (scratched cornea). I carry Neurosporin Opthalmic ointment. You'll need a prescription from your doctor to obtain it.
- Fishhook in the skin. I carry injectable Xylocaine but have never needed it. Learn the painless string pull method of removing a fishhook if you plan to fish.

Add the usual complement of gauze and tape, Tylenol, aspirin, bandaids and antacid. A fire-making kit consisting of a flattened milk carton, some cedar shavings, fine kindling, a candle, and chemical fire starter will help combat the cold.

BASIC TRAINING

Training is fun for everyone and especially rewarding for the leader. I start by showing all the old Bill Mason *Path of the Paddle* films, which are available from most public libraries in 16 mm or video cassette. Sometimes I photocopy selections from the canoeing literature and assign them for homework. The kids enjoy learning about hypothermia, first aid, and camping procedures. As the trip nears, plan an overnight shakedown cruise, or at least several practice sessions.

ETHICS

Explain backcountry ethics *before* you take to the woods so every youngster understands the ecological concerns behind the them. Leaders must model every rule and adopt an uncompromising attitude towards any practice that might harm the environment. School them in the ways of how to make camp, cook, wash, and "go to the bathroom" in the woods. Kids want to be part of the solution to pollution, and they will willingly follow your lead.

Kids also will be curious about their wilderness hosts—the fish, frogs, chipmunks, deer, and yes, bears! Teaching kids to respect wildlife is integral to instilling a general respect for nature.

Unfortunately, most educational material on wilderness ethics is geared to adults. You'll have to simplify. I introduce the subject by giving the ethics quiz in Appendix 3. We discuss the quiz, then see a short slide show that details various backcountry abuses.

HOW TO PLAN YOUR ROUTE

Kids may plead for a week of layover days so they can swim and socialize, but inwardly they want the physical challenge of a real canoe trip. A fifteen-mile day, or six hours on the water, is a good daily goal. One "gut buster" day followed by a subsequent layover day should be included to meld the group. Begin at dawn; finish near sundown. Paddle hard and choose tough portages that will wear everyone out. That night rekindle the day's events over a crackling fire and bottomless pots of soup and hot chocolate. Laze back, watch shooting stars, and tell stories until exhaustion overwhelms. Then snooze until 10 A.M., serve a lazy pancake breakfast, and dedicate the rest of the day to swimming, fishing, and exploring. Or, place each kid on a barren rock for a three-hour isolation experience. At first they'll react negatively to the idea, but afterwards they'll pressure you for more. Most teenagers have never been alone (or quiet!) for that long in a wilderness environment. This will be one of their most meaningful experiences.

WHEN IT RAINS

Scenario: The last two days of your trip have been hot and sunny; you've been making good time and are, in fact, ahead of schedule. This morning, you awake to a cold, persistent rain. You should (a) sleep in and take your layover day here or (b) rouse 'em up now and get paddling!

The correct answer is B. Worst thing imaginable is a bunch of grumbling kids massed under the rain tarp with nothing to do.

If you think you have problems now, try ten hours of confined, unplanned activity! Feed 'em well, dress 'em warm, and work 'em hard. They'll respond enthusiastically and with the understanding that you have their best interests at heart. Later, when the sun returns, you can stop and spend the day. Kids find plenty of ways to entertain themselves when the weather is cooperative.

DELICATE CONCERNS

Seemingly insignificant things like how and where to go to the bathroom really frustrate teenagers. So, develop rules that everyone understands. For riverside rest stops I simply point and say, "Girls upriver, boys go thataway." Co-ed overnights, however, require more finesse! If there's a unisex latrine, you'll need a policy that provides for privacy.

I simply hang the nylon bag that contains the toilet paper in a conspicuous place at the edge of camp. When someone needs to use the facility, he or she simply takes the bag and goes. No one is to use the latrine until the TP bag returns. If the latrine is visible from camp, you should rig a privacy screen. I often carry an old nylon tarp for this purpose.

Before the trip the girls should be taken aside and told how to dispose of sanitary napkins. The excitement and intense physical activity may cause some girls to menstruate early or to have painful cramps. A wise leader is sympathetic and understanding, and he/she carries appropriate medication.

THE INEXPERIENCED LEADER

In case you've forgotten, there are eighteen kids going on this canoe trip. That's nine for you, nine for the inexperienced youth director. Granted, your colleague means well, and he's willing to learn, but he is not proficient in the bush. Nonetheless, he is responsible for nine kids. How can you smooth the way for him without affecting the social structure of his group?

At camp: Camp far enough apart so the groups can't see or hear one another, but close enough so you can help should an emergency arise. To retain individuality, each crew must operate on their own. So except on planned occasions, *do not* let kids from one camp socialize with those from another. I cannot stress this point enough! Remove kids from the rules and social order of their own group and they'll create endless problems.

On the water: Locating portages often calls for resourcefulness, patience, and good map-reading skills—attributes that your inexperienced colleague is just beginning to learn. To allay your friend's fears, suggest a time to start the next day's paddling. Then, at the appropriate hour, cruise by his campsite and casually signal him to follow. Stay close enough to instill confidence but distant enough to prevent socializing. Continue visual contact throughout the day, breaking off for lunch and to camp. After a day or two of this your friend will have his sea legs and you can go your separate ways.

SAFETY

Continually stress safety. Admonish kids to slow down and look where they're going when carrying a canoe or pack. Nearly all accidents are the result of hurrying a task or packing an oversize load. A particularly dangerous practice is "double packing" (carrying two packs, one on the back, the other on the chest), which obscures your view of the trail and your feet.

RULES

Kids are apt to forget items of equipment when they portage or break camp. So establish a foolproof system that makes every item accountable. Everyone should commit the following rules to memory:

1. Everyone, regardless of swimming ability, must wear a life jacket when canoeing or lining canoes.
2. Take life jackets inside your tent when you retire. Do not sit on them or throw them around! No one wants to wear a PFD that has been left in the mud or rain.
3. Before retiring, canoes are turned over and tied to a tree so a high wind won't turn them into a kite. The first time you chase an empty canoe down a bleak river in the black of night you'll understand the importance of this rule.

As you can see, canoeing with teens is an exercise in commitment. At times you'll be mother, father, doctor, and teacher. You'll have to find ways to include

CANOEING AND CAMPING

unpopular kids in group activities and to get the rest of the crew to accept them. Occasionally, you may even have to give up the shirt on your own back to warm that of a child.

Rewards? You bet! I've paddled dangerous whitewater and remote rivers north of the Arctic Circle. I've stood among thousands of caribou and have even been charged by grizzlies. But nothing warms my heart more than the tearful hugs and "Thanks, Cliff," that I receive at the end of a canoe trip.

Canoeing with teens helps me to rediscover the forgotten innocence of being young.

CHAPTER FOURTEEN

Wilderness Navigation

The Fond du Lac River begins in the northwest corner of Saskatchewan at the far end of Wollaston Lake. It is described by Eric Morse (author of *Canoe Canada*) as a "remote challenging river for expert whitewater canoeists." The Fond du Lac is all of that and more, though getting to the river is the hardest part of all.

First, there's the bone-jangling ride over the Mississippi Tote Road—two hundred miles of fist-sized gravel that is guaranteed to fully depreciate the toughest vehicle. Then there's the thirty-mile crossing of Wollaston Lake—a sprawling piece of water with hundreds of islands and bays to confuse you. The Fond du Lac begins innocently in an obscure bay at the northwest corner of the lake. All you have to do is find it!

The trip sprang from an assignment for *Canoe* magazine—one whose article deadline came just five days after our scheduled return. No way could I knock out a story that fast. I'd have to do some writing en route and find a way to shorten our time on the river.

The solution was to hire a tow from Wollaston Lake Lodge to the mouth of the Fond du Lac. That alone would save two days of paddling. The tow would cost us seventy Canadian dollars; but no matter, we'd come to run the river, not fight wind and waves.

We unloaded our gear at the Wollaston dock, packed the canoes, and tied them to the waiting motor boat. The sandy-haired man who was to guide us to the river seemed amiable enough. He was a college student from Toronto—a crackerjack fishing guide who purportedly "knew the lake blindfolded."

Within minutes we were waterborne, skimming northward at full throttle.

Casually, I looked at my map, then nudged my friend beside me. "Look here, Darrell…this guy's going the wrong way, too far east. Whatcha think?"

"Aw c'mon, Cliff; he's the guide! Keep the faith, friend!"

"Yeah…okay."

With that I folded my map contentedly and simply watched the scenery pass. Ultimately I heard a coughing sound that suggested we were out of gas. No problem; our guide shut down the twin Mercs and plugged in the auxiliary tank. Then he quietly drew forth a tiny Xeroxed copy of a 1:500,000-scale map of the area and squinted boldly at it.

"Hey, this guy's really a pro," I muttered to my friend. "Look at that map. Man, I'd need bifocals just to tell the water from the land!"

There was a long silence. Then came a sheepish grin and the words, "Any of you guys know where we are?"

I looked at Darrell and together we burst out laughing. Our guide was *lost!*

Reluctantly, I pulled out my detailed 1:50,000-scale map and stared intently at it. "I dunno," I replied, "but one thing's certain; we're too far east!"

After that, it was merely a matter of intensive map study and fancy compass work to determine our location. Within the hour we chugged confidently to the hidden bay that marked the Fond du Lac—no thanks to our "expert" guide.

As this case illustrates, anyone can get confused on a complex waterway, even when it is "familiar turf." The wilderness has a delightful way of humbling the most confident of egos. The remedy is to carry a good map and compass and to become expert in their use.

EQUIPMENT

Maps

Topographic maps can be purchased by mail from the sources below.

For United States topographic maps, write:

> United States Geological Survey
> Box 25286, Federal Center
> Denver, Colorado 80225

Order Canadian maps from:

> Canada Map Office
> Department of Energy, Mines and Resources
> 615 Booth Street
> Ottawa, Ontario, K1A 0E9

For charts and tide tables of United States coasts, the Great Lakes, and sections of major rivers, write:

National Ocean Survey
Division C44, 6501 Lafayette Avenue
Riverdale, Maryland 20840

Canadian charts and tide tables are available from:

Hydrographic Chart Distribution Office
Department of Fisheries and Oceans
1675 Russel Rd., P.O. Box 8030
Ottawa, Ontario K1G 3H6

Request a free "Index to Topographic Maps." This index will tell you what maps are in print, in what scale, and the cost. If much of your travel will be on large, complex lakes, request the largest scale available. Maps in 1:24,000 scale are best for picking your way across mazelike lakes, although at this large scale you'll need several of them. Smaller 1:50,000-scale maps are ideal for most wilderness canoe travel (the larger the denominator of the scale, the smaller the actual map scale). Usually however, you can't afford to be so choosy. Large-scale maps are readily available for heavily traveled or civilized areas, while more remote sections of the continent may be available only in small scale. Avoid maps with scales smaller than 1:250,000 (1 inch = 4 miles). Such small-scale maps are useful to experts, but they don't inspire confidence in beginners.

When you have secured your maps, mark the route with a colored "hi-liter" and number each map sheet in the order you will use it. To save weight and bulk, trim off and discard all unprinted margins. I prefer to coat nonwaterproof topographic maps with Thompson's Water Seal—an industrial-strength compound used for sealing wood and concrete block. Every hardware store has it. A single light coat of TWS, applied with a foam varnish brush, makes maps reasonably waterproof and allows you to write on them, Or, for a waterproof seal cover maps with clear contact paper. If you like more stiffness to your map, purchase some Chartex dry-mounting cloth for the backing from Forestry Suppliers, Inc., 205 West Rankin Street, Jackson, Mississippi 39204. Forestry Suppliers has a number of navigational aids that you might find useful. Their catalog is free.

Map Case

A map case is essential, whether maps are waterproof or not. Plastic map cases take a lot of abuse on canoe trips, so get something sturdier than a Ziploc bag. If your canoe is properly outfitted with shockcords as explained in chapter 2, your map case can be secured by sliding it under a shockcorded thwart. When you encounter rapids, stuff the map into your nylon thwart bag for the ultimate in security.

The Compass

The most versatile and suitable compass style for the canoeist is the orienteering model. Orienteering compasses have built-in protractors that allow you to quickly

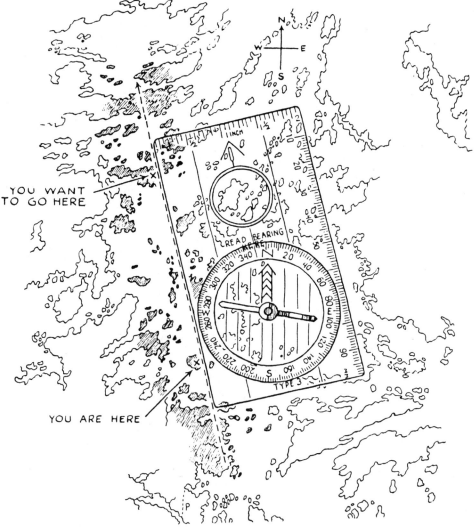

YOU WANT TO GO HERE

READ BEARING HERE

YOU ARE HERE

To determine the bearing of a point on your map:
1. Place the left or right edge of the compass over your position in line with your destination.
2. Hold the compass base steady and turn the needle housing until north on the *dial* points to north on the map (top of the map).
3. Read your bearing at the index (350 degrees in the illustration). Note that the magnetic needle is not used for this computation!
4. Now, remove the compass from the map and turn it (turn your body with the instrument) until the north end of the magnetic needle points to the north on the dial. You are now facing in a direction of 350 degrees. Simple, isn't it?

Figure 14-1 Orienteering compasses have built-in protractors that allow you to quickly and accurately compute directions from a map without first orienting the map to north.

and accurately compute direction and scale distance from a map without first orienting the map to north. This means you can define a precise direction—to the nearest degree—while sitting in your bobbing canoe. The direction is physically set on the compass by turning a dial, so there's nothing to remember or write down.

To determine the bearing of an object with an orienteering compass, point the compass at the object and, while holding the base steady, rotate the graduated housing until the north end of the magnetic needle points to N (north) on the dial. The direction you are facing, in degrees, is locked onto the compass dial and can be read at an index inscribed on the base. The compass can then be slipped back into your pocket for reference later. And you don't have to remember the direction that was set on the compass, either, since it will remain positioned on the dial until you turn the housing. To verify your direction with this style of compass, merely point the instrument away from your body and rotate your body and the compass until both ends of the magnetic needle points to N on the dial.

Since you don't have to read the numbers set on the dial, orienteering compasses are ideal for use at night or under conditions of rain or poor visibility.

Hint: Strap a small wrist compass around a thwart or seat frame and you'll be able to check directions without fumbling for your pocket compass.

Although all good compasses come with adequate instructions for average use, you should have an in-depth understanding of basic navigational principles if you intend to engage in serious route finding. For a thorough treatment of navigational procedures, see my book *Basic Essentials of Map and Compass,* published by ICS Books.

At the end of this chapter there is a practice map that you can use to test your route-finding ability. If you can successfully complete the map exercise, you are ready to set out on a wilderness trip on a reasonably complex waterway.

First the Basics

The compass is graduated in degrees. There are 360 degrees in the compass rose. The cardinal directions (north, south, east, and west) are each 90 degrees apart. The northeast (NE) quadrant encompasses the direction from 0 to 90 degrees, the southeast (SE) quadrant from 90 to 180 degrees, and so on. Learn to think in quadrants. Before determining the precise direction you wish to travel, ask yourself, "In which quadrant am I traveling?" This will help eliminate the most common of compass errors—the 180-degree error. For example, if your map tells you to go southwest and your compass points to 45 degrees (NE quadrant), you know something is wrong; you are facing 180 degrees in the wrong direction. It is not uncommon to transfer data from map to compass and make serious directional mistakes. A knowledge of your approximate direction of travel should be known *before* you get down to the specifics.

Using the map of Lost Lake on page 147 (figure 14-6), assume you are at point A. You want to go just north of point H and take the portage trail to the South Arm of Maze Lake. A glance at the map tells you to begin heading northwest until you hit the shoreline, then to follow it around until you pass Bays

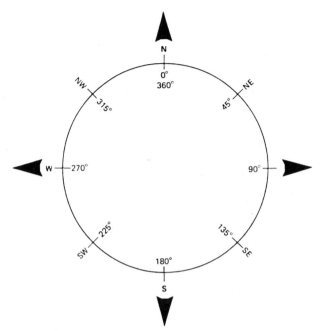

Figure 14-2 The Compass Rose

1 and 2, then on into Bay 3, and straight to the portage. Very simple, right? Wrong! Look at the map scale. You won't be able to decipher islands from mainland or one bay from another. When you look out across a lake of this size and complexity, you will see green as far as the eye can see. Physical features will blend with one another until the entire landscape is one of sameness. Because of wind and waves you will lose all sense of distance traveled. You can rely on your watch for a rough estimate, but it will be difficult for you to judge whether you have completed two miles or three. You can easily bypass Bay 3, or you can get completely turned around and become convinced that a channel between islands is a large bay, or vice versa.

One of the greatest tragedies of twentieth-century canoeing occurred because of a map misinterpretation. In 1904 Leonidas Hubbard, Dillon Wallace, and George Elson attempted to penetrate the interior of an unexplored part of Labrador. "How vividly I saw it all again," said Wallace later on. "Hubbard resting on his paddle and then rising up for a better view, as he said, 'Oh, that's just a bay and it isn't worthwhile to take the time to explore it. The river comes in here at the end of the lake. They all said it was at the end of the lake.' And we said, 'Yes, it is at the end of the lake; they all said so,' and went on." The Susan River they wrongly ascended was a dead end. With provisions gone and winter setting in, the expedition ended at Lake Michikamau, many miles from their destination.

Hubbard, weakened by hunger and exhaustion, could not continue. He died on Sunday, October 18, 1904. His two companions, Elson and Wallace, retraced their fateful steps down the Susan Valley to civilization. We will never know why Hubbard, a man of experience, did not take the time to check his map and compass at such a critical point in his journey.

Using Compass and Map for Precision Direction Finding

In order to keep track of where you are on a body of water of any size, you must know, within reason, your position at all times. This means you must proceed along an established direction, or bearing as it is called.

Assume you have begun a canoe trip at point A on Lost Lake (see the map of Lost Lake at the end of this chapter). You plan to paddle the full width of the lake and portage into the South Arm of Maze Lake, which lies just to the west. Horseshoe Island, you've heard, has an excellent campsite on its south end (point B), so you decide to make your first camp there. You choose to paddle straight to the campsite rather than take the longer, more confusing route around the shoreline to your west. To accomplish this, you will need to determine the *exact* direction (bearing) in degrees from point A (your location) to point B (your destination).

You can use your orienteering compass or a simple protractor for this computation. To use an orienteering compass, place either the left or right edge of the compass base plate on point A. Place the forward edge of the same side of the base plate on point B. Your compass is now pointing in the direction you want to go—from A to B (not from B to A). While holding the base plate tightly in position, turn the compass housing until north on the dial points to the top (north) of the map. **Caution:** Don't use the magnetic needle! Your direction of travel—292 degrees—is now locked onto the dial and can be read at the index inscribed on the compass base. Now, while holding the compass in front of you with the direction-of-travel arrow inscribed on the base pointing *away* from your body, rotate your body and compass (you may have to turn the canoe to do this) until the magnetic needle points north on the dial. You are now facing in the proper direction. Locate a notch or visible incongruity on the horizon that you can identify as being on this course of travel. Put your compass away and paddle toward your objective. Do *not* attempt to watch the compass needle and paddle at the same time! In time your objective (point B) will pop into view and you will have found your campsite.

Once you have reestablished your position at point B, you can continue your voyage to C, then to D, and so on. In this manner you can cross a large, complex waterway without fear of becoming lost, for you will know where you are all the time.

Aiming Off

Assume you are at point G and you want to locate the portage to South Arm just north of H. There are three portages leading out of Bay 3, but only 1 goes to

South Arm. Since 1 degree of compass error equals 92.2 feet per mile (tan. 1° x 5,280 feet), even a slight error can be disastrous.

From G to the South Arm portage is about three miles. A 4-degree error over this distance would cause you to miss the portage by at least 1,100 feet, or nearly one-fourth of a mile. You would, in effect, be lost, since you'd have no idea which direction to go to find the portage. Instead, "aimoff." Determine the bearing from G to a point just south of the portage—in this case, point H. Locate a notch on the horizon that corresponds to the bearing you have computed and start paddling. When you reach the shoreline, you will be somewhere near H, although you may be a few hundred feet north or south. But one thing is certain— you are south of the portage to South Arm. You merely have to paddle up the shoreline (north) until you come to the portage. This principle of aiming off is equally useful on land or for locating the mouth of a river. By aiming off you minimize the possibility of error.

Declination

A compass points (actually, it doesn't point—it lines up with the earth's magnetic field) to *magnetic* north, not *true* north. This angular difference, called *declination*, must be considered whenever you use your compass (see figure 14-3 and 14-4). In the eastern United States the declination is westerly and in the western United States the declination is easterly. If you live right on the imaginary line that goes directly through both the true and magnetic north poles (called the *agonic* line), your declination will be zero.

If you live east or west of the agonic line, your compass will be in error, since the true north pole is not in the same place as the magnetic north pole. As you can see from the declination chart, the farther away you are from the agonic line, the greater the declination. Moreover, the magnetic north pole is constantly moving, so declination varies from year to year as well as from place to place. To find the exact declination for your area, consult a topographic map or call a

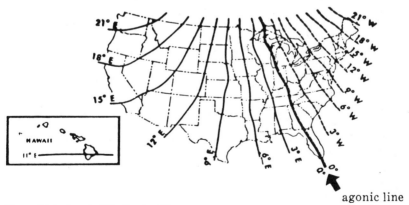

agonic line

Figure 14-3 Standard Declination Chart

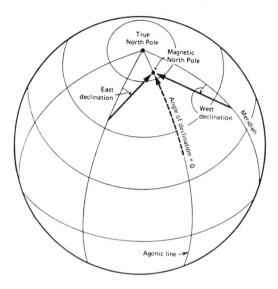

Figure 14-4 Compass Declination: The angular difference between *true* north and *magnetic* north (the direction the compass points).

surveyor. In the continental United States declination can range from 0 degrees at the agonic line to more than 20 degrees in New England and the far west. Unless your canoeing will be limited to those states very close to the agonic line, you will have to consider declination.

The easiest solution to the declination problem is to purchase a compass that can be adjusted for declination. Many orienteering models have this feature. Or you can compute magnetic variation mathematically, according to the following rhyme: *Declination east—compass least* (subtract east declination from your map direction): *Declination west—compass best* (add west declination to your map direction).

Maps are almost always drawn in their true perspective (any variation is so small that it can be ignored). So when you determine a direction of travel or bearing from a map, it is a *true bearing*. The true bearing taken from your map will have to be converted to a *magnetic bearing* to be set on your compass.

Assume a declination of 10 degrees east. Applying the rhyme "declination east, compass least," subtract 10 degrees from the true bearing computed from your map. In the Lost Lake map exercise a true bearing of 292 degrees from A to B would equal 292 degrees minus 10, or 282 degrees, using the declination given above. Conversely, if declination were 10 degrees west, it would be added (292° + 10° = 302°), and this value would be set on your compass. If this is confusing and you plan to travel in areas where the declination is large, you would be well advised to spend the extra money for a compass that can be manually adjusted for declination.

CANOEING AND CAMPING

Position by Triangulation

Suppose you find yourself on a large, mazelike lake where you can identify two or more topographical features but you don't know exactly where you are. Finding your position by triangulation is simple with an orienteering compass (or you can use a protractor with a more conventional compass). Pick out one point on the horizon that you can identify—Old Baldy in this case (see figure 14-5). With your compass shoot a magnetic bearing to the point (bearing = 312 degrees). Change this magnetic bearing to a true bearing by reverse application of the rhyme (312° + 6 = 318°). Draw the *back* (reciprocal) bearing (318° - 180° = 138°) through Old Baldy, using your compass base plate and a sharp pencil. (When using an

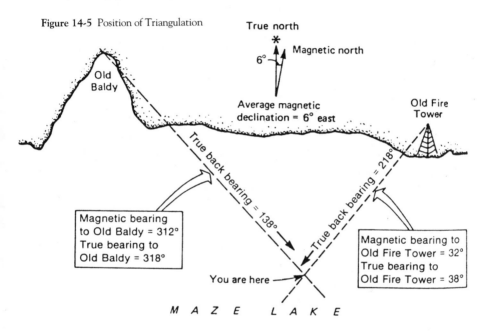

Figure 14-5 Position of Triangulation

True north

Magnetic north

6°

Average magnetic declination = 6° east

Old Fire Tower

Old Baldy

True back bearing = 138°

True back bearing = 218°

Magnetic bearing to Old Baldy = 312°
True bearing to Old Baldy = 318°

Magnetic bearing to Old Fire Tower = 32°
True bearing to Old Fire Tower = 38°

You are here

M A Z E L A K E

orienteering compass, you don't have to compute the back bearing at all.) Set 318 degrees on the compass dial, place your pencil point on Old Baldy, and put the forward edge of one side of your compass base plate against the pencil point. Rotate the entire compass in an arc around the pencil until north on the dial (not the needle) points to the top (north) of the map. **Caution:** Do not turn the compass housing during this operation, since the true bearing that you just computed to Old Baldy (318 degrees) is set on the dial. This procedure will *not* work if you change the dial setting! Using the base plate as a straight edge, draw your line. Repeat the exercise using another point on the horizon that you can identify (the old fire tower). You are located where the two lines cross. For greatest precision you may wish to take three sightings.

Navigation At Night

Canoeing by moonlight on a slow-moving river or calm lake is an enjoyable experience. However, no canoeist's repertoire is complete until he or she has done some black-night travel by compass. Some years ago while canoeing in Minnesota's Boundary Waters Canoe Area, I was awakened to find three bears in camp—mama and two babies. In spite of previous stern warnings, the youth group that I was guiding had left food scattered around the camp. The dehydrated fruit that was on the lunch menu evidently had had a superabundance of prunes, and the youngsters had elected to have a prune fight. Even after a thorough policing of the grounds, enough prunes remained to attract the bears. We blew whistles, banged on canoes, clanked pots and pans, and made a variety of other noises in the hope of frightening away the hungry bruins, but to no avail. Our bears were used to people. After they knocked down one tent, we became convinced it was time to leave, and within a few minutes we put to sea. The night was black as pitch, but locating a new campsite without a moon to guide us was not difficult. We set course by compass and located a new site within an hour. My compass, a Silva Ranger, had a good luminous night-sighting device.

Lost Lake Exercises

Referring to the map of Lost Lake (figure 14-6), assume you are at point A. Using your compass or a protractor, determine the bearing and approximate time of travel from point to point. Proceed alphabetically, ending your trip at the portage into South Arm. Assume a travel speed of two miles per hour. When you have finished and your answers check, work the triangulation problem below.

Triangulation Problem

You can identify Dunker Hill at a magnetic bearing of 256 degrees and Kaby Lookout at a magnetic bearing of 4 degrees. Where are you located? Clue: Don't forget to apply the declination.

Answer to Triangulation Problem

You are located at the north end of Horseshoe Island.

Answers to Lost Lake Exercises

Point	True Bearing	Distance (miles)	Approximate Travel Time	Magnetic Bearing (to be set on your compass)
A to B	290°	2¾	1½ hours	284°
B to C	341°	1½	¾ hour	335°
C to D	15°	⅖	20 minutes	9°
D to E	338°	4	2 hours	332°
E to F	274°	3 ¼	1½ hours	268°
F to G	244°	1 ⅛	½ hour	238°
G to H	227°	2 ½	1¼ to 1½ hours	221°

H to portage (paddle north up the shoreline to portage): Time - about 15 minutes.

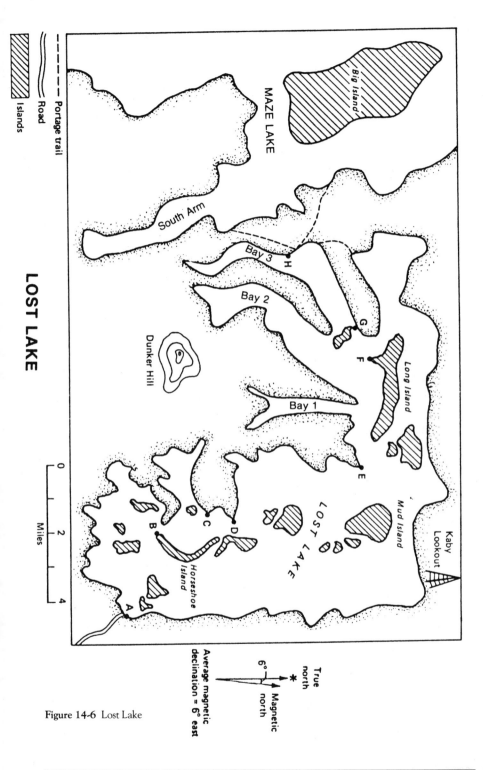

Figure 14-6 Lost Lake

River Navigation and Trip Guides

No discussion of canoe routefinding would be complete without mentioning trip guides and river navigation. With the impact of man on river systems, it is becoming more and more important for the prospective river paddler to know what the water conditions are like before setting the canoe in the water. Many local and even far northern rivers are now dam controlled and are very dangerous at high water or impossible at low water. Barbed-wire fences strung across rivers maim and kill canoeists each year, and the people who string these fences generally have the law on their side. Each year we read about canoeists who inadvertently paddled over a dam because they didn't know it was there. If you paddle rivers, you must be able to accurately locate and identify dams, rapids, fences, and other obstacles in the water that can endanger your trip.

Unlike lake navigation, it is very difficult to fix your position on a river. A compass will be useful for rough directions only. You can reaffirm your location at major river bends, identifiable rapids, or incoming streams. On wilderness canoe trips where it is necessary to ascend an incoming stream and thereby change watersheds, a high degree of resourcefulness and competency in map reading may be required, especially if there are many streams to confuse you.

Lastly, some of the best maps of river conditions are the local people who live in the area. Always check with them before embarking on a river, even if you have run it many times. Many things may have changed since your map was drawn. Although you should heed the advice of local persons, bear in mind that most don't understand canoes. Locals have a tendency to exaggerate the dangers of their rivers. Nevertheless, they will provide you with much good information. Especially seek out foresters or professional people who work in the area. Outdoors people will generally tell it like it is, or at least they will exaggerate less.

PART FOUR

Camping Skills

CHAPTER FIFTEEN

Quick Fixin's

A compendium of luscious fast food ideas for those who'd rather canoe than cook

BREAKFAST

Seven A.M. and breakfast in the backcountry. Yesterday, you served scrambled eggs and diced/fried Canadian bacon. Today there is instant oatmeal, dehydrated fruit, and leftovers from the day before. On hand is one egg and a cinnamon bagel apiece, a quarter pound of "still okay" bacon, and a fist-sized chunk of cheddar from Monday's lunch. Hmmmm. Why not forget the gruel and wow 'em with "Egg McBagel" and fruit stewed in sugared rum?

You pump some air into the cold steel tank of the PEAK 1, then adjust the valve to a gentle simmer. The magic of your culinary talents are about to be unveiled. But the first order of business is to make some gourmet coffee.

How to Make Gourmet Camp Coffee

Use the very best fine-ground coffee. Add a scant pinch of salt to your coffee pot and bring the water to a rolling boil. Remove the pot from the heat source and add one heaping tablespoon of coffee per cup. If you want cinnamon-flavored java, toss in about ¼ teaspoon of cinnamon for every eight cups of brewed coffee. For almond- or mint-flavored coffee add an equivalent amount of liquid extract to the brew. Stir once to mix everything, snap on the lid, and set the pot near the fire. Do not allow the coffee to boil! Doing so will kill and bury a fine brew. Allow the grounds to settle for three minutes, then pour off the sludge at the spout. Now, lie back and contemplate what you've been missing at home.

To make "Northwoods Egg Coffee," mix the grounds with beaten egg (use just enough egg to thoroughly moisten all grounds). Bring water to a rolling boil, then drop in egg-saturated grounds. Immediately turn heat to simmer. Simmer very gently (do not boil!) about five minutes. Then, remove from heat and add a dash of cold water to settle grounds. The result is a clear, rich coffee everyone will rave about.

For an added treat, fill your coffee cup with premixed cocoa powder and top off with fresh-made camp coffee. The result is class-act cinnamon, mint, or almond mocoa, served steaming hot in the heart of the backcountry.

Rum (Brandy) Stewed Fruit

Ingredients: One package of mixed evaporated fruit; 1/4 teaspoon cinnamon; 2 heaping teaspoons of brown (preferred) or white sugar or honey, or you may substitute sugared cherry or apple-flavored drink crystals; one or two shots of your favorite liquor.

Cooking procedure: Place all ingredients and enough water to cover into a small pot with tight-fitting lid. Bring to a boil and simmer for fifteen minutes or until fruit is tender. The result will excite the stogiest crew!

Egg McBagel

Each Egg McBagel requires about two minutes to make. First, fry the Canadian bacon—Thirty seconds per side in a good hot pan will do the trick. (*Note:* Vacuum-sealed Canadian bacon will keep at least a week in the heat of summer. American slab bacon will last almost as long. For extended trips try Celebrity-brand canned bacon, which never spoils.)

Drain the bacon on a few sheets of paper toweling and set it aside. Lubricate your skillet with a squirt of vegetable oil and fry the egg (break the yoke) on one side. Opposite the egg, place the two bagel halves face down. Cover the pan immediately and use low heat. After thirty seconds, flip the egg.

While the egg is cooking, place a slice of Canadian bacon on the face of one of the bagel halves and flake some cheese on top. Top with the well-done egg. Add the other bagel half to complete the sandwich, cover the meal for thirty seconds or until the cheese melts. Ferret your Egg McBagel onto an awaiting plate and chow down.

LUNCH IDEAS

The ideal canoe lunch is tasty, nourishing, compact, lightweight, crushproof, immune to spoilage, and can be consumed on the run. If you can't unwrap it, slice it, spread it, or spoon it from a can, forget it. When the weather howls bloody murder, you may consciously cheat and prepare instant soup or hot, sweet tea on your gasoline stove. But the traditional fire-brewed shore lunch of fishing guides is out of place on the typical canoe trip—that is, if you'd rather canoe than cook.

On my early canoe trips I relied exclusively on high-tech crackers like Rye-Crisp and Wasa Brot, on which I heaped oily synthetic cheeses that came in cardboard boxes and squeeze tubes. A poly bottle of peanut butter, another of jam, and a stick or three of beef jerky constituted lip-smacking traveling fare. For lengthy trips above the tree line, where even foodstuffs must succumb to the precept of "ruggedness," I trashed the crackers in favor of traditional pilot biscuits. If you're not familiar with these once-popular shipboard staples, suffice it to say that, contrary to popular belief, they can indeed be broken. All you need is a full-sized axe and a good head of steam!

Despite years of prenatal dependence on this nutritious fare, I now gag at the thought of ever consuming it again. Indeed, I have asked Manitou to strike me dead if another pilot biscuit or squish of tube cheese ever again creases my lips.

The noon repast should be politely civilized. The humble bagel provides the nucleus of the meal, at least for a day or three. Bagels lack preservatives, so they grow harder by the hour, ultimately sprouting a rich green growth of penicillium after a week out. Vacuum sealing helps (inexpensive units are available), but not enough. Figure on a maximum shelf life of three days and you can't go wrong.

Pita (Mediterranean pocket) is avowedly my favorite lunch bread. The ones sold in Mediterranean food shops are by far the tastiest, but these usually lack preservatives and so keep only about as long as bagels. You'll find additive-packed pitas, which will last two weeks or more, on the refrigerator shelves of most large supermarkets. Again, vacuum sealing markedly increases shelf life.

No need to rely on plastic-tasting synthetic cheeses. Good block cheddar, Colby, or Monterey Jack will keep at least two weeks in the heat of summer. Cheese should be vacuum sealed or wax coated to ensure freshness over the long haul. Simply trim surface mold when (if) the need arises.

I abandoned beef jerky long ago in favor of "Barrel O'Beef" brand summer sausage and Cervalot. There are other tasty meats that don't require refrigeration. Ask your grocer about them.

There's no substitute for good jam. I'll drive fifty miles to get the best Canadian preserves. What's good at home is great afield.

To the above items add a stash of chunky peanut butter and a favorite granola, salted nut roll, or fruit bar. (Have you tried Cotlets, Aplets, and Grapelets?) A splash of mustard will turn your meal into an adventurous picnic.

ON INTO SUPPER

Scenario: For three days you've been pinned in a quiet cove by an icy, thirty-mile-an-hour wind. It's only the first week out and you've already exhausted the two-day supply of extra rations you brought along for just this purpose. Should you should put your crew on half rations? Not if you can creatively conserve food without cutting down. The following "Dumpling Soup" recipe provides an alternative.

Ingredients: Instant soup, any flavor; Minute Rice; Bisquick; cheese; dehydrated hamburger or canned chunk chicken, if you have it.

Cooking procedure: Add 20 percent more water than called for in the soup directions. Fail to do this and you'll have glue, not stew! Bring the soup mix and water to a boil, add one cup Minute Rice for every four servings, then drop marble-sized Bisquick dumplings into the stew. Add dehydrated hamburger and

---

meats at the start of cooking. Simmer five minutes or until dumplings are done. Add up to one-fourth pound cut-up cheese during the last minute of cooking. Hmmmm good!

Note: You can beef up food value and "environmental effect" by adding noodles, spaghetti, or elbow macaroni. Potato buds can be used as a stock thickener or to make tasty dumplings. Pancake batter and fish breading can also be pressed into service for this purpose. Try diced, fried summer sausage (lunch leftovers) in your dumpling stew.

Note: Dehydrated hamburger provides the basis for dozens of trail meals— spaghetti, chili, Stroganoff, or tacos, to name a few. A simple, low-cost dehydrator is all you need. *Procedure:* Brown and drain the hamburger, then pour boiling water over the meat (optional) to remove as much grease as possible (the water will strip some nutrients). Place ground beef on a dehydrator tray lined with several thicknesses of paper toweling. Dry at 140 degrees Fahrenheit for twelve hours or until hard. Most folks can't tell dehydrated hamburger from fresh when it is used in stews and sauces.

Tip: To make dumplings without soiling your hands, pour batter and water into a Ziploc bag. Seal the bag and knead the contents until they are mixed. Cut a slit in the bag bottom and squeeze the mix—use the bag like a cake decorator— into the soup. Afterwards, burn the bag.

HORS D'OEUVRES

Pita melt. Slice each pita in half and fill the cavity with cheese chunks and garlic flakes. Lightly brown the pita in olive oil (preferred) or margarine in a covered skillet. Superb!

Baked fish fillets. This mouth-watering entrée is the invention of Bill Marcouiller, a wilderness canoeist from Battle Lake, Minnesota. Serve as an hors d'oeuvre or full meal.

Ingredients: Split fillets of your favorite fish; margarine; salt and pepper; ½ teaspoon dehydrated parsley flakes; 2 tablespoons of diced, fresh onion; ⅛ pound or more of your favorite cheese; 1 teaspoon bacon bits.

Preparation: You'll need to rig an oven of some sort. Set the fillets on a thin layer of margarine, then smother them with more margarine, salt, pepper, dry parsley flakes, and onion. Cover the oven and bake ten minutes or until done. When the fillets are nearly cooked, spread cheese over them and add bacon bits on top. A dash of garlic flakes livens flavor. Bake until cheese is melted. You won't believe how good this is.

Popcorn. Adjust your stove to medium-high heat and barely cover the bottom of your largest cooking pot with vegetable oil. Add a half- dozen kernels of the best (I use Orville's) popping corn to an uncovered pot. Don't add salt to the popper as this encourages sticking and burning. When all the "maidens" have popped, the oil is at the right temperature. Add enough corn to cover the pot bottom, no more. You'll have tough popcorn if you don't allow steam to escape during the popping process, so find some way to vent the pot cover. Continuously shake the pot with a twisting motion until the cover is forced away from the pot, then immediately pour out the popped corn into a large paper grocery sack. Season with margarine and fine-grade popcorn salt. Shake the paper bag to mix.

MEAL MANAGEMENT

Remove all excess packaging (like cardboard boxes) on foodstuffs and repack each meal separately in a large Ziploc bag. If you place plastic bags in color-coded nylon stuff sacks (I use green for breakfasts, yellow for lunches, red for suppers), you'll avoid much pack groping at mealtime.

Each packaged meal should be a complete unit. It should not be necessary to search for sugar, instant milk, or cocoa. All items should be premeasured in the correct amount necessary to serve the group.

The best way to pack breakables and crushables like crackers, candy bars, and cheese is to place them inside rigid cardboard containers (milk cartons are ideal). Place onions, green peppers, and other vegetables in a paper or cotton sack and carry them inside your coffee pot.

COOKING GEAR

For a party of four you'll need three nested pots with covers, a coffee pot or tea kettle, and a Teflon-lined skillet. Most skillets sold in camping shops are awful. Get a standard 10-inch "Mirro" with Silverstone finish and make a removable handle for it.

Each person should have an insulated cup, plastic bowl, and spoon. A stainless-steel Sierra cup makes a great ladle.

Tips: A graduated plastic pitcher tied to a canoe thwart will become a handy bailer if your canoe takes on water. Use the pitcher for mixing instant drinks and measuring water for soup. Store silverware and spices in a fabric utensil roll that can be snapped or tied to an overhead line (figure 15-1). When rains come, run a tight line just beneath your cooking fly and hang your utensil organizer from it. Now, everything you need to prepare meals will be clean and at hand. Package a few sheets of paper toweling with breakfast and supper meals. The towels are handy for drying cookware and cleaning the stove.

OVENS

In the days of large campfires I used a folding reflector or dutch oven for all my baking. Now, however, I cook almost exclusively on a stove, so my baking methods reflect this bias. An oven constructed of a large ring aluminum gelatin mold (figure 15-2) provides excellent results. To use the gelatin mold for baking on your stove:

1. Grease the mold and pour your bake stuff into the outside ring. Decrease the suggested amount of water by up to one-fourth for faster baking.
2. Bring the stove to normal operating temperature, then reduce the heat to the lowest possible setting. Center the mold over the burner head, top it with a high cover, and relax. Cooking times are about the same as

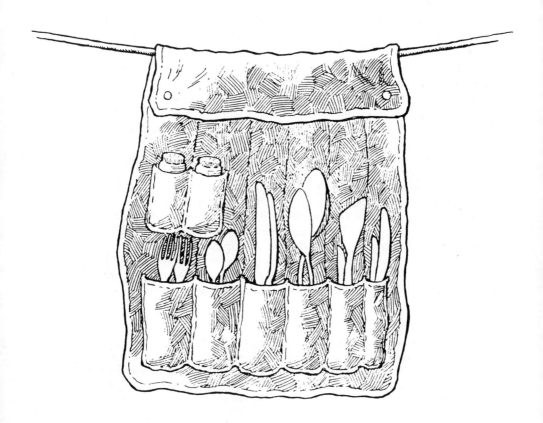

Figure 15-1 When rains come, hang your fabric utensil roll from a tight line string beneath your cooking fly. Now, everything you need to prepare meals will be clean, dry and instantly at hand.

those suggested in the baking directions.
3. Cool the mold by setting it in a shallow pan of water for a few minutes.

The triple-pan method of baking works well on a stove or fire. You'll need two nesting skillets, a high cover, and a half-dozen small nails or stones.

1. Evenly scatter the nails or stones onto the surface of the large (bottom) frying pan.
2. Place your bake stuff into the small frying pan and set it on top of the nails (the two pans must be separated by nails or stones to prevent burning).
3. Cover the unit and place it on your stove. Use the lowest possible blue-flame setting. *Warning:* Don't use this method with a thin aluminum skillet on the bottom; you'll burn a hole right through it!

Figure 15-2 The "Gelatin Mold" Oven: It works on any trail stove.

SANITATION

For short trips where there are few portages, all garbage should be bagged in plastic and packed out of the wilderness. When this is impractical, as on lengthy outings, the best method of disposal is to burn it in a good, hot fire. Please pick aluminum foil out of the flames before it melts all over everything!

In populated areas fish entrails should be buried well away from the campsite and at least 100 feet from water. In remote areas they may be left for sea gulls on a large boulder, *well away from human habitation.*

Human waste should also be buried, preferably under a four- inch cover of soil to maximize decomposition. Burn toilet paper and sanitary napkins and carry a water bottle to be sure flames are dead out!

And please, don't throw food—or anything else—into Forest Service box latrines or chemical toilets. Bears commonly upset latrines to get at the food they want!

Dishes should be washed on land, well away from the water's edge. Greasy dishwater is best poured into a small hole in the ground and covered with soil.

WATER PURIFICATION

Most authorities recommend that you boil, filter, or chemically treat all water taken from a questionable source. That's sound advice, providing you have the necessary chemicals and/or equipment plus the self-discipline to use them. Although I occasionally boil (160 degrees Fahrenheit will kill almost everything) my drinking water on backcountry trips, I confess to laziness in this respect. As often as not, I drink untreated water, but I am very careful where I get it. Here are the guidelines I religiously follow:

- Go well away from shore to get your drinking water. If you are camping at a spot that is frequented by man or animals, go upstream of the source to get your water. On lakes a minimum of 150 feet from shore is recommended.
- Decay organisms (bacteria and protozoa) generally prefer the shallows, so the deeper your water source, the better. On large lakes I often weight a cooking pot with a rock and let it down 30 feet or more by rope. Avoid any water that has a green or greenish brown color. Water with a green tinge contains algae and is usually loaded with microorganisms.
- Don't take water from backwaters and stagnant areas. These are breeding places for microbes.
- Don't take water near beaver dams or lodges. Beaver are the favored host of Giardia lamblia—a small protozoan that will make you plenty sick!

A FINAL THOUGHT

As you paddle the rivers of North America, you will surely come upon thoughtless people and their refuse. Tin cans, bottles, mattress springs, car bodies, and worn-out appliances are but a sampling of the debris I've observed in my travels. Once, in the Boundary Waters of Minnesota, I was awakened at midnight by an enterprising trumpeter. On another occasion a teen group sang ribald songs the whole night through. Many times I've put out other people's campfires and cleaned their trashed fire places and campsites. But my efforts are not unique: everyone who cares about the future of our wild places follows suit throughout each and every camping trip. Doing battle with environmental idiots is a never-ending, nonrewarding process.

Nearly everyone who paddles America's rivers ultimately develops a profound respect for them and an abiding disdain for those who abuse them. Nonetheless, it's important to realize that those who violate the backcountry usually do so out of ignorance, not willful disrespect. To this end, I offer the suggested "Backcountry Ethics Quiz" in Appendix 3. Use it as you wish. Reproduce it in any number you like, and share it with as many people as you can. Education may not be the total answer to eliminating environmental abuses, but it is a start.

CHAPTER SIXTEEN

Weathering the Storm

I pitched the old Eureka Timberline tent on a gentle knoll amidst a clump of birch trees. There was a much better spot about 20 feet away—a well-worn site where hundreds of tents had stood before. But the barren place was in a slight depression that was devoid of ground cover—a good rain could mean a flooded tent. Besides, a long-dead spruce tree, its limbs poised menacingly overhead, stood nearby waiting patiently for the first big wind to send it crashing down.

At about seven P.M. it began. Slowly at first, with a gentle rain that lasted an hour. Then the storm intensified; soon rain fell in thick sheets, driven by hurricane-force winds of sixty miles an hour!

For a while I just stood complacently in the prestorm drizzle and watched the chilling blackness expand across the sky. Then, methodically, I began to make necessary adjustments.

First I pulled a coil of parachute cord from my pack and strung two taut guy lines from each tent peak to trees nearby (the Eureka Timberline is self-supporting and theoretically does not need to be guyed). Then I weighted each stake with heavy rocks that I dragged from the streambed below.

Within minutes it struck. The big Eureka shook and groaned as the initial swish of the wind tore at her. But she stood fast.

The heaviest part of the storm passed quickly, but a steady forty- to fifty-miles-per-hour wind continued unrelentingly throughout the night.

We awoke the next morning to the scene of disaster. Trees were down everywhere. The dead spruce lay about where I predicted. And every depression was overflowing with water. Smugly, my wife and I exchanged glances. We'd weathered the storm!

Admittedly, stormproofing a camp requires luck as well as skill. Really, what would I have done if that clump of birch hadn't been there? Or if rocks or brush prohibited placing the tent on high ground?

It's unrealistic to expect any woodland tent to withstand sustained winds of over forty miles per hour, regardless of how you pitch it. But rain is another matter. A sophisticated expedition tent that's pitched badly or set in the wrong spot is sure to admit water, while a simple forest tent that's rigged correctly won't. In the end your skills at coping with the weather are much more important than your gear.

KNOW THE SHORTCOMINGS OF YOUR TENT AND CORRECT THEM

Blowing rain or groundwater is most likely to enter a tent through ground level or exposed perimeter seams. Obviously, all tent seams should be waterproofed— either with a special seal glue or liquid compound. (I prefer "Thompson's Water Seal," a brush-on chemical formulated for waterproofing concrete floors. TWS is flexible and stable in all temperatures and is available at most hardware stores. The product is also useful for waterproofing maps and clothing.) And, of course, no tent floor will remain impervious to water forever. The solution is to always use a plastic groundsheet inside the tent. Water that wicks through the floor will then be trapped beneath the ground cloth and you sleep dry.

Some "experts" suggest that you place the groundcloth under the floor to save the floor material from abrasion and puncture. You'll really have a sponge party if you follow this advice, as groundwater will become trapped between the plastic sheet and floor and be pumped (the weight of your body creates a pressure differential) into the tent!

The use of an *interior* groundcloth is the best wet-weather tip I can give you. It will also reduce the number of holes and abrasions in your tent floor.[6]

The best way to improve the wind-stability of any tent is to run twin guy lines from each peak. Extend the lines outward at 45-degree angles to the poles. Don't mess with the original tent guy. What you want is three lines emanating from each end of the tent. Whenever possible, attach guy and stake lines to an immovable object, such as a tree or boulder. Or, weight stakes with rocks or logs so they won't pull out when the ground softens from a rain.

Next, attach loops of ⅛ inch shockcord to every stake and pole loop (the extra guys are added only during a storm, but the shockcord loops should be a permanent part of your tent's anatomy). The elastic loops will take the wind stress normally reserved for the tent's fabric and stitching.

At home take a hard look at your tent's design. Pitch it tightly on level ground and check out the lay of the fabric. If you have an inexpensive tent, there'll probably be some sag along the roof line. You can string out the ridge so it doesn't luff, but only at the expense of the base. If the fly sags along its border (looks as if it needs more stake loops to support it), it probably does. Get out your

---

[6] If you don't believe this, begin a trip with a new plastic groundsheet in your tent. At trip's end, count the number of holes in it – holes which would otherwise have been in your tent floor!

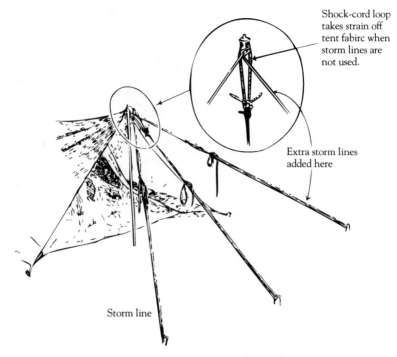

Shock-cord loop takes strain off tent fabirc when storm lines are not used.

Extra storm lines added here

Storm line

Figure 16-1 Stormproofing the tent.

sewing machine and add them—as many as necessary to make the fabric drum tight and wrinklefree. Use the storm loops like you'd use reef lines on a sailboat— only in rough-weather emergencies.

While you're handy with the needle and thread, reinforce questionable stitching, especially at the corners and peak of the tent. Afterwards, carefully waterproof all the seams you've sewn!

The RainFly

Waterproofing and windproofing your tent is only half the solution to weathering a storm. The other part is providing a dry place to cook and relax. Customize your nylon rain tarp by sewing five equally spaced nylon loops to one side (figure 16-2). These loops provide anchor points for rigging cords and allow you to pitch the tarp in a variety of geometric configurations. Be sure to reinforce all the loops with a backing of strong fabric. And remember to seal all the seams you sew.

Rigging procedure. The majority of campers are pretty haphazard about fly pitching, and, as a result, the first good wind that comes along rips the corner grommets right out of the fly. Consequently, some canoeists believe that tarps should never be set up in a wind-driven rain. Unfortunately, that is when you need their protection most.

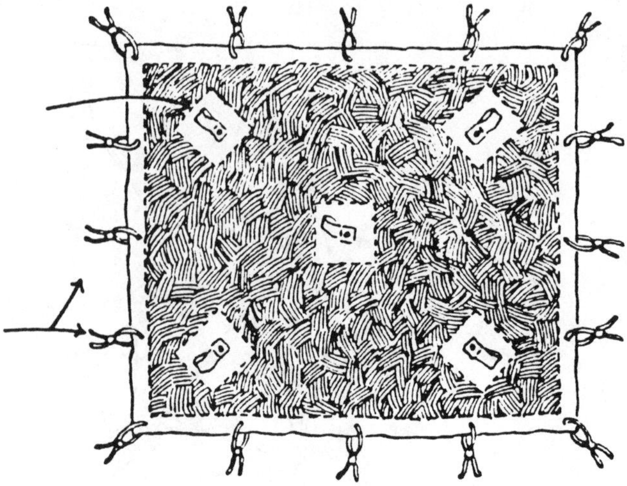

Add five loops on face of fly. Reinforce loops with heavy material on back side

Add additional ties if necessary—there should be at least five ties per side.

Figure 16-2 Customizing the Rain Tarp: Add ties to all the grommets and sew five equally spaced loops to the face. This will allow you to pitch the tarp in a variety of geometric configurations.

After years of experimenting I've come to prefer this simple, strong and efficient method of rigging (figure 16-3).

Materials. A fly customized like the one shown in figure 16-3; 50 feet of nylon rope; six lightweight aluminum tent stakes; two trees, not over 30 feet apart.

1. Locate two trees about 15 to 20 feet apart. String a drum-tight line between the trees about 5 feet off the ground. Use two half-hitches at one end of the rope and a power-cinch with a quick release knot at the other end (see chapter 10 for a review of knots).

2. Take the pair of ties at one corner of your fly and wind one tie of the set around the rope in a clockwise direction. Take at least four turns around the rope. Secure the ties with a simple overhand bow.

3. Pull the other corner of the open end of the fly tight along the rope and secure it with the ties, as in number two above. The wrappings will provide sufficient tension to keep the corners of the tarp from slipping inward along the rope when the fly is buffeted by wind.

4. Secure all remaining ties to the rope with a simple overhand bow. (By securing the fly at several points along the length of its open end rather than just at the corners, as is commonly done, you distribute the strain across a wide area, thus increasing the strength of the fly.)

5. Go to the back of the fly, pull it out tight, and stake.

6. Run the center cord over a tree limb or a rope strung just above and behind the fly. Snug up the center cord (use a power-cinch with a quick-release knot) to pull the center of the fly out. Add additional lines if necessary.

CANOEING AND CAMPING

7. Secure the sides of the fly with extra cord. Complete all knots with a quick-release loop. You now have a sturdy, rain-free shelter that won't flap in the wind. Total rigging time? Under three minutes!

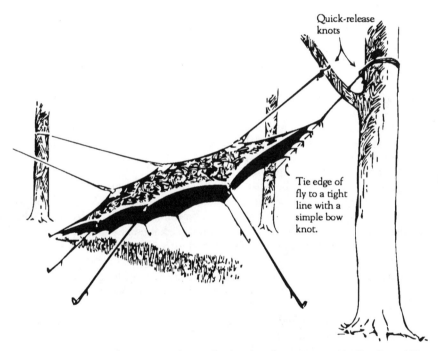

Quick-release knots

Tie edge of fly to a tight line with a simple bow knot.

Figure 16-3 A customized rain tarp can be rigged in less than three minutes and will withstand 30-mile-per-hour winds.

CHAPTER SEVENTEEN

Bugs, Bears and Bothersome Beasts

A ttitude is everything! Gear yourself for the worst, repeat frequently, "Bugs don't bother me; bugs don't bother me," and you'll retain a measure of sanity in insect country. But mix a bad attitude with "incorrect" psychology and the pesky critters will devour your hide!

Beyond psychology there is science and the usual array of preventative measures. Topping the list is a *small* head net. Bulky, military styles with drawcord hems that button down to breast pockets are a nuisance in canoe country where head nets are put on over life jackets. A simple rectangular swath of netting that in a flash can be wadded to fist size and stuffed into a hat crown or shirt pocket is best.

Protecting your torso is another concern. A layer of long underwear, worn tight against the skin, discourages most bites, except on exposed ankles and wrists, which are easily protected by daubing on DEET-laden repellent. Your armor is complete when you've tucked your pants into high-topped boots and sealed shirt-cuff openings with mating strips of Velcro.

You'll also want to consider "color" when choosing field clothes. Tans, grays, greens, and powder blues neither attract nor repel insects, but darker shades of blue, black, or deep red drive insects buggy. Navy blue is by far the worst color you can wear in the bush.

Tips: (1) To keep pesky insects away from your face, dribble a generous supply of DEET on your cotton bandanna, then tie the hanky around your neck. (2) After the bite Benadryl is the best nonperscription medication you can buy for allergic reactions.

HOW TO BEARPROOF YOUR CAMP

Ask any newcomer to the Boundary Waters Canoe Area what he or she fears most about camping out, and you'll hear "bears!" Some folks are afraid they'll be eaten alive; others are worried that a bear will get their food. And backcountry managers offer small consolation, for their advice is often predicated on outdated conditions.

For example, here are some suggestions from U.S. Forest Service publications that are distributed to canoeists who enter the BWCA. All except one will get you into trouble. Can you tell which one?

1. Hang your food pack from a tree limb that is at least 10 feet off the ground or suspend it from a horizontal pole set between two trees. Some campsites have a "bear pole" that everyone uses. Please leave the pole as you found it as a courtesy to the next person who occupies your site.
2. Don't leave food in your tent!
3. Leave tent flaps open so that a bear can walk in and check the place without resorting to brute force.
4. This recommendation comes from the canoeing literature: Place food under an overturned canoe. Pile some pots on top to function as a night alarm system.

If you said number 2, you are correct. All the rest are wrong—dead wrong! Here's why: Consider number 1: Bears are creatures of habit whose behavior is programmed by past experience. They quickly learn where and in what campers put food.

For example, I once saw a black bear tear apart a pack that was filled with sleeping bags and tents. This pack had never been used for food, so there was no odor. Past experience robbing other camps had taught this bear that food comes in packs and packlike objects. It was the *shape* of the container that attracted the bear, not the smell! Same with tin cans, which they learn about at the local dump. How else can you explain why bears will bite through sealed tin cans that have no food smell on them?

Bears also learn that food packs grow on trees! *Certain trees.* On popular campsites there is usually only one tree with limbs that are high enough to discourage a determined bear, and invariably every camper suspends his food pack from this tree. "Soon as it gets dark, I'll climb up there and get it," thinks the bear. Consider this scene—which I witnessed some years ago:

A big sow bear and two youngsters waddle into camp and make a beeline right for the "bear tree." The food pack is hanging from a limb, maybe 12 feet up and 3 feet out. Mama sidles up to the tree trunk, stretches out, and begins to climb. She goes up a few feet, then slides down. She's ticked. Real ticked! So she woofs and snaps as she circles the tree, her eyes fixed on the dangling morsel.

Meantime, one of the cubs gets wind of the food and starts to climb. Six feet up, it stops and begins to bawl. Seconds later, mama shimmies to the rescue and nudges junior's behind. The kid scoots the remaining distance, stretches out on the limb, and hooks a pack strap. Seconds later, the cub and pack fall to the ground and everyone enjoys a tasty meal, courtesy of some camper who "followed the rules."

Moral? Tree your food if you like, just don't use the same tree as everyone else!

Next, let's check out number 3—*leave your tent flaps open so a bear can walk in.* This one dates back to the 1950s when campers cooked fresh foods on open fires within yards of their canvas tents. Cotton holds odors tenaciously and a curious bear might just check them out. So it probably was wise to leave the door flaps open so a bear could look around without tearing the place apart.

But nylon tents and fire don't mix, so now we pitch our shelters—and do all our cooking—out of range of windblown sparks (and food odor). Modern campers know better than to cook or eat around their tents, and bears know better than to waste their time looking for food in places that in the past have not been productive.

Closed tent flaps *will not* discourage a black bear, but they will keep out insects, snakes, and the weather. The feds should've trashed this idea long ago!

Now, let's address number 4—*Place food packs under an overturned canoe and set pots on top as a night alarm system.* This idea dates back to the days when campsites were not so heavily used and before camp bears became "conditioned" to the ways of man. Today's camp bears are well educated. They're not afraid of man, woman, or clanging pots. A man told me a big black bear once tried to get at some food stored under his aluminum canoe. When the bruin couldn't connect, he began to jump on the craft. Damage included a broken seat and several pulled rivets. Just think what he could have done to a Kevlar canoe!

Now that we've shown that traditional rules don't work, here is a nontraditional one that does: *Break the classical conditioning habit: don't put your food in the same place as everyone else!*

I simply take food packs out of the immediate camp area and place them in the woods or along the shoreline, taking care to keep them well away from game trails. Then I separate packs by 50 feet or more for additional security. Bears don't see very well, especially at night, so as long as there's no food odor, they'll leave things alone.

All of which brings us to the matter of a clean camp. Leftovers should be burned or buried well away from camp and water. Every spaghetti noodle and grain of popcorn must be gathered and disposed of. The feds are right about number 2: Bears will tear down your tent to get at food!

Let's review the rules for bearproofing your camp:

1. Seal all foodstuffs in plastic so there is no odor.
2. Break the classical conditioning habit by putting your food where others don't.
3. Don't keep food in your tent. In grizzly country the cooking area should be at least 100 yards from where you sleep!
4. Keep a scrupulously clean camp and you'll find that what works for bears also works for ground squirrels, mice, and birds.

WHAT TO DO IF A BEAR COMES INTO CAMP

Stay calm. It's your food he wants, not you. Over the years I've confronted a number of black bears, and my nonchalant procedure goes something like this: First I yell or blow a whistle. A wild bear will hightail it at the sound, but an experienced camp bear won't even look up. Secure in the knowledge that my food has no odor and is out of sight beyond the camp boundary, I maintain a safe distance and watch the show. After the bear checks all the usual places and finds nothing, he will move on in search of more productive fare.

Again, let me emphasize that you *will not* scare off a determined camp bear with screams, whistles, or cherry bombs. He will leave only when he's sure there is no food around!

On the other hand, don't be too laid back. There are crazy bears like there are crazy people. You could run into one with an injury or with a nasty disposition. Unprovoked bear attacks are rare, but they do happen. So stay cool, keep your distance, and identify a getaway route in the unlikely event that things get out of hand.

During the summer of 1987, a man was mauled by a small black bear in the Boundary Waters Canoe Area. She followed him into the lake and kept chomping away. Fortunately, he survived the mauling. When Forest Service personnel later killed the bear, they discovered she was starving!

If you are confronted by a black bear, stretch out your arms (so you'll appear as big as possible) and firmly call, "WHOA BEAR, STOP MONSTER," or something that suggests you're in command. Do not run! Black bears are mostly bluff. A "charging" bruin will almost always stop within a few feet of you, then turn tail and run.

If you are attacked by a black bear, *don't* play dead! Research suggests that if you fight, you'll probably live to tell about the encounter.

GRIZZLY ENCOUNTERS

In 1984 I was "charged" by three grizzlies on the Arctic tundra. As they galloped towards me, I dropped to the ground and played dead, certain that the ploy would become fact in a matter of seconds. The bears came within two canoe lengths, then wheeled off into the highlands. I later learned from a wildlife biologist that my behavior was textbook perfect.

Note that you respond to a grizzly attack by *playing dead*. If attacked by a black bear, *fight like hell*!

In summary, to keep your food safe from bears: (1) Keep a clean camp and don't store food in your tent; and (2) Store odor-free food packs where other people don't. If you tree packs, don't use the same tree as everyone else.

As mentioned, I never hang my packs in bear country. But I keep a scrupulously clean camp, and at night I put my food in an unsuspecting place. I've lived by these simple rules for thirty-five years, and in that time neither I nor anyone in my charge has ever lost food or equipment to any animal. And that, friends, is the "bear" truth!

Canoe Terminology

Aft: Toward the stern (back) end of the canoe.

Amidships: The center or middle of the canoe.

Bailer: A scoop (usually made from an empty bleach jug by cutting off the bottom) for dipping accumulated water from the bottom of the canoe.

Bang plate: On aluminum canoes, a curved metal plate running from deck to keel. Holds the metal skin together and takes the bangs. The bang plate is called the stem band on canoes of wood-canvas construction.

Beam: The widest part of the canoe. Generally occurs at or slightly aft of the waist (middle) and just below the gunwales.

Bilge: The point of greatest curvature between the bottom and side of a canoe.

Blade: The part of the canoe paddle that is placed in the water.

Bow: The forward (front) end of the canoe.

Bowman: The forward or bow paddler (whether male or female).

Broadside: A canoe that is perpendicular to the current of a river, thus exposing its broad side to obstacles in the water.

Broach: To turn suddenly into the wind.

Carry: To carry a canoe and gear overland, either to a distant watershed or to safer water. **Carry** is synonymous with **portage**.

Deck: Panels at the bow and stern that attach to the gunwales.

Depth: The distance from the top of the gunwales to the bottom of the canoe when measured at the beam (sometimes called **center** depth, as opposed to the depth at the extreme ends of the canoe).

Draft: The amount of water a canoe draws.

Flatwater: Water without rapids, such as a lake or slow-moving river.

Flotation: Styrofoam or other buoyant material set into the ends, along the inside bilges, or beneath the decks and gunwales of aluminum and fiberglass canoes to make them float if upset. Can also mean any buoyant material, such as life jackets, beach balls, and inner tubes.

Footbrace: A wood or metal bar against which a paddler braces his feet. Footbraces help secure the paddler in the canoe and so add to the efficiency of his strokes.

Fore (forward): Toward the front end (bow) of the canoe.

Freeboard: The distance from the waterline to the top of the gunwales at their lowest point. The greater the freeboard, the greater the ability of the canoe to handle rough water, assuming the canoe is well designed.

Grab loop: A loop of rope that passes through the hole or painter ring at each end of the canoe. Gives you something to "grab" when you capsize.

Grip: The top end of the shaft of a canoe paddle, where you grip it.

Gunwales (pronounced "gunnels"): The upper rails of the canoe.

Hogged: A canoe with a bent-in keel.

Inwale: That part of the gunwale that protrudes into the inside of the canoe.

Keel: A strip of wood or aluminum that runs along the center of the canoe. Keels prevent lateral slippage in winds and protect the bottoms of canoes from damage in rocky areas. However, their main purpose is to stiffen the bottom of a canoe (see Keels: Friend or Fiend on page thirteen for the complete lowdown). There are two types of keels in common use: **Standard, fin, or tee keel**—a deep keel that extends up to and inch or more into the water. An ideal choice where travel will be limited to large, windy lakes: **Shoe (whitewater) keel**—a rounded or flat strip of metal or wood designed to protect the bottom of a canoe from damage. The smooth contours of shoe keels allow water to flow over them with little resistance. Thus they permit quick turns in rapids.

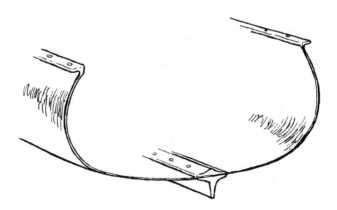

Standard or tee keel for use on windy lake only.

Leeward: A sheltered or protected place out of the wind. In nautical terms, leeward is the direction toward which the wind is blowing.

Line: Rope used to tie up a canoe or pull it around obstacles in the water. Also refers to working a canoe downstream around obstacles in the water with the aid of ropes (lines) attached to the bow and stern.

Outwale: The part of the gunwale that protrudes over the outside of the canoe hull. Outwales are desirable for canoes that will be used in whitewater, as they help deflect spray when the bow of the canoe plunges in rapids.

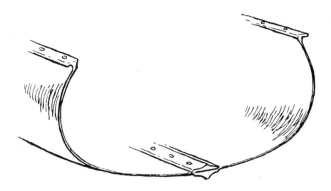

Canoes with shoe (whitewater) keels are more maneuverable and are less likely to catch on subsurface rocks than similar models with standard keels..

Painters: Lines attached to the bow and stern of a canoe.

Planking: Lightweight boards nailed to the ribs on wood-canvas canoes. Planking runs perpendicular to the ribs of a canoe. Its main purpose is to support the canvas.

Portage: see *Carry.*

Ribs: The lateral supports that run at right angles to the keel on the inside of a canoe. Ribs provide hull rigidity and structural strength and are necessary on aluminum and wood-canvas canoes. The trend is away from ribs in canoes of modern construction, as the new synthetics are very strong and do not require crossbracing for support.

Rocker: An upward curve of the keel line of a canoe. When placed on a level surface, a canoe with rocker will, like a rocking chair, rock up and down (fore and aft). Canoes with rocker turn more easily than those without rocker.

Rock garden: A shallow place in a river that has many scattered rocks.

Seats: Generally, there are two seats in a canoe. They may be made of wood, fiberglass, plastic, or aluminum. Wood-framed seats, which are strung with cane or nylon webbing, and tractor-type molded fiberglass seats are most comfortable. Aluminum seats are least comfortable and get cold in cool weather. For greatest warmth (and comfort) cover aluminum seats with waterproof foam and secure the foam to the seats with waterproof tape. You spend long hours sitting in a canoe; consequently, more than a passing consideration should be given to the seats.

Sliding seat: A canoe seat that can be moved forward or aft to adjust trim. Most of the best canoes now feature sliding bow seats as a standard or optional accessory.

Skid plate: A piece of thick Kevlar that is glued to the bottom ends of Royalex canoes. Prevents abrasion of the vinyl skin of the canoe. Skid plates are a desirable addition to Royalex canoes that will be used in shallow, rocky rivers.

Skin: The outer covering of the canoe. May be wood, canvas, aluminum, or other material.

Splash cover: A fitted cover designed to keep water out of a canoe. Splash covers are useful in rough rapids and big waves. Even small, sporty canoes are suitable for wilderness use if they are covered.

Spray deck: An extra-long deck equipped that a cowling to deflect water that comes over the ends of a canoe.

Spray skirt: A waterproof fabric sleeve that is attached to the splash cover at one end and is secured around a paddler's waist by means of elastic shock cord at the other end.

Thwart: A cross brace that runs from gunwale to gunwale. Thwarts give strength and rigidity to the hull.

Toe blocks: A feature of whitewater canoes. Wood or foam blocks glued to the canoe's bottom support the paddler's feet and keep him from sliding around in the boat while maneuvering.

Thigh straps: A feature of whitewater canoes—a webbing harness that runs from the gunwale or seat frame through a ring on the canoe's bottom. The paddler pushes his knees tight against the straps to "lock" them in place—a very secure arrangement, especially when combined with "toe blocks."

Tracking: Working a canoe upstream, against the current, with the aid of ropes (lines) attached to the bow and stern.

Trim: The difference in the draft at the bow from that at the stern of a canoe. A properly trimmed canoe will sit dead level in the water. Trim can be adjusted by weighting the bow or the stern.

Tumblehome: The inward curve of the sides of a canoe above the waterline.

Tumpline: A strap that is secured just above a person's forehead to help support a pack or canoe.

Waist: The middle of the canoe.

Waterline: The place to which the water comes on the hull of the canoe when it is set in the water.

Whitewater: Foamy (air-filled), turbulent water.

Yoke: A special crossbar equipped with shoulder pads for portaging the canoe.

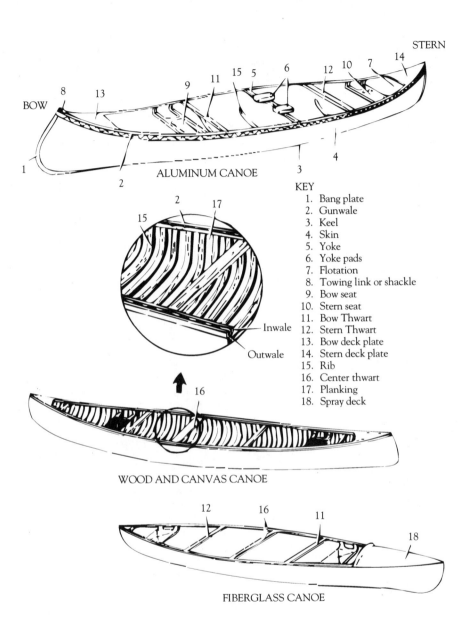

BOW

STERN

8 13

15 5

6

10 7 14

11

12

9

1

2

ALUMINUM CANOE

3

4

KEY

2 17

15

Inwale

Outwale

16

1. Bang plate
2. Gunwale
3. Keel
4. Skin
5. Yoke
6. Yoke pads
7. Flotation
8. Towing link or shackle
9. Bow seat
10. Stern seat
11. Bow Thwart
12. Stern Thwart
13. Bow deck plate
14. Stern deck plate
15. Rib
16. Center thwart
17. Planking
18. Spray deck

WOOD AND CANVAS CANOE

12 16 11

18

FIBERGLASS CANOE

Types of Canoes

Equipment List for Two People for a Trip of One Week or More

GROUP EQUIPMENT

- tent (preferably with self-supporting framework)
- plastic ground cloth for use *inside* tent
- coated nylon cooking fly, 10 feet X 10 feet or larger
- three Duluth style packs (#3 size), or two Duluth packs and a pack basket or "Wanigan."

- waterproof liners for packs
- 100 feet of 3/8-inch nylon rope
- one all-steel hand axe in sturdy sheath
- one compact folding saw
- repair and miscellaneous kit: one small pliers with wire cutter, one roll fine copper wire, silver duct tape, needles, thread, instant epoxy, 12-inch square of fiberglass cloth for canoe or paddle patching, six hammer-driven rivets, two aluminum carbiners, one nylon pulley, small file for sharpening the axe, whetstone and honing oil, 3-inch square of scrap canvas for repair, small piece of leather for repair, sharp sewing awl, safety pins, sandpaper

- six heavy-duty rubber ropes with steel S-hooks attached
- large sponge for bailing
- cook kit and oven
- graduated 2-quart plastic shaker
- biodegradable soap and abrasive pad for dishwashing
- stove and gasoline
- matches in waterproof container; cigarette lighter

- several candles
- first-aid kit (See *Wilderness Medicine* by Dr. Bill Forgey for a complete list of first-aid items and their use.

INDIVIDUAL EQUIPMENT
- life jacket
- two paddles
- Sleeping bag and foam pad
- two pairs of military field pants (choose wool pants in spring and fall)
- two light weight, long-sleeved shirts
- one medium-weight wool or pile jac-shirt or three sweaters
- one cotton T-shirt
- one pair of long johns (spring and fall trips)
- four pairs wool socks
- one light nylon wind parka (not waterproof)
- one waterproof two-piece rain suit
- one brimmed hat for sun; wool stocking cap for chilly days; sou'wester hat for rain
- extra glasses if you wear them and security strap for glasses
- three changes underwear
- one small towel
- two cotton bandannas
- one pair rubber-bottom boots
- one pair canvas sneakers or other soft footwear for camp use
- one pair lightweight leather or polyester gloves. For arctic trips use leather-faced wool, Gore-Tex, or neoprene gloves
- one flashlight, extra bulb, and batteries
- sheath knife or heavy-duty pocket knife
- toiletries (include hand lotion for chapped hands)
- orienteering compass
- map set in waterproof case
- insect repellent
- insect head net (essential for trips into northern Canada, otherwise unnecessary

Backcountry Ethics

Here's a not-so-simple quiz that will test your understanding of backcountry ethics. Answers and rationale follow. Hint: Some questions have more than one right answer, and some answers are "open to interpretation."

I hope you'll duplicate this quiz (permission is granted by the publisher) and share it with friends, with church and Scout groups, with fishermen, hunters, birders, hikers, canoeists, and with everyone who cares deeply about the future of our wild places.

NEGLECT AND THE PROPER WAY

Questions

1. The best way to dispose of fish entrails is:
    ____ (a) Throw them into the river or lake
    ____ (b) Bury them at least 100 feet from water
    ____ (c) Leave them on a prominent rock (well away from camp area) for seagulls
    ____ (d) They are biodegradable so it makes no difference how you dispose of them.

2. To properly dispose of human waste:
    ____ (a) Bury it at least 12 inches deep, 100 feet from water
    ____ (b) Human waste degrades quickly; it should not be buried!
    ____ (c) Bury it 4 to 12 inches deep, at least 100 feet from water.

3. It's okay to dispose of biodegradable wastes (food scraps and such) in Forest Service outhouses, box latrines, and chemical toilets:

____ (a) True
____ (b) False
____ (c) Open to interpretation.

4. What's the correct way to dispose of steel and aluminum cans?

____ (a) Burn them out, pound them flat with the back of an axe or rock, and pack them out in a strong plastic bag.
____ (b) Burn them out, then bury them!
____ (c) Bury them at least 100 feet from water.
____ (d) Any of the above methods are acceptable.

5. How should you dispose of glass bottles in the backcountry?

____ (a) Break them into fine pieces and bury them.
____ (b) Pulverize them to a powder and bury them at least 100 feet from water.
____ (c) Burn them out in a hot fire then bury them.
____ (d) If you bring bottles into the backcountry, pack them out!

6. To keep water from entering your tent in a heavy rain, dig a shallow trench around it so the runoff will drain harmlessly away.

____ (a) True
____ (b) False
____ (c) Open to interpretation.

7. If you have a small amount of uneaten food, toss it into the bushes. Animals will dispose of the food quickly and completely.

____ (a) True
____ (b) False
____ (c) Open to interpretation.

8. It's okay to construct log benches and tables at your campsite as long as you use cord, not nails.

____ (a) True
____ (b) False
____ (c) Open to interpretation.

9. Best way to dispose of aluminum foil is:

____ (a) Bury it
____ (b) Burn it
____ (c) Pack it out
____ (d) Any of these methods is satisfactory.

10. It's okay to play loud radios during daylight hours.

____ (a) True

_____ (b) False
_____ (c) Open to interpretation.

11. Pounding nails into trees so you'll have places to hang things, improves the campsite for the next party.
    _____ (a) True
    _____ (b) False
    _____ (c) Open to interpretation.

12. Leave your axe or hatchet at home: It is not essential to your comfort or survival.
    _____ (a) True
    _____ (b) False
    _____ (c) Open to interpretation.

13. Bright-colored equipment—canoes, tents, packs, and clothing—detract from the "wilderness experience." Choose "earth tones" instead.
    _____ (a) True
    _____ (b) False
    _____ (c) Open to interpretation.

14. You may bathe and wash clothes and dishes in a waterway as long as you use biodegradable soap.
    _____ (a) True
    _____ (b) False
    _____ (c) Open to interpretation.

15. Always bring a strong plastic bag for garbage...and PACK OUT the contents!
    _____ (a) True
    _____ (b) False
    _____ (c) Open to interpretation.

16. Use a campstove for all your cooking. It is unethical to build fires in wilderness areas.
    _____ (a) True
    _____ (b) False
    _____ (c) Open to interpretation.

17. You are responsible:
    _____ (a) To check the remains of your fire by hand before you leave the area; if ashes are hot enough to burn your hand they're hot enough to burn a forest!
    _____ (b) To bring the right gear and clothing for the worst conditions you may encounter.
    _____ (c) To help others who are in trouble.

_____ (d) To educate others in the "proper way" to treat wilderness areas

_____ (e) All of the above.

18. Ecology-minded outdoorspeople will row or paddle rather than use motors. The noise of motors frightens wildlife and the oil/gasoline scum and carbon-monoxide exhaust is harmful to fish and aquatic organisms.

_____ (a) True

_____ (b) False

_____ (c) Open to interpretation.

19. To insure a restful sleep, the wise camper will always place evergreen boughs or a bed of green leaves beneath his or her sleeping bag.

_____ (a) True

_____ (b) False

_____ (c) Open to interpretation.

20. You are responsible to call unsafe and illegal practices that you observe to the attention of the person(s) involved...and to report violations of land- and water-use regulations to the appropriate authorities (if practical).

_____ (a) True

_____ (b) False

_____ (c) Open to interpretation.

Answers

1. B is correct, though C is acceptable if (1) you are in an area where seagulls are common, and (2) the waterway _is not_ heavily fished.

2. C. The top foot of soil contains the greatest number of decay organisms (bacteria and fungi), so breakdown will occur most rapidly in this area. The idea is to bury wastes deep enough so animals won't dig them up, yet shallow enough so they'll decompose quickly.

3. Absolutely false! Garbage should be buried or packed out, never thrown in latrines. Bears commonly upset latrines to get at food buried among the human waste. The mess that results is indescribable!

4. A is correct. Steel cans degrade in around seventy-five years. Aluminum cans require hundreds of years! Cans should _always_ be packed out!

5. D is correct. It may require one million years for a glass bottle to "return to nature." For this reason, bottles should always be packed out! Better yet, they should _never_ be brought into the backcountry!

6. False! Trenching creates soil erosion. It is unethical and in most places, illegal to ditch tents. Use a plastic ground cloth inside your tent and you'll stay dry in the heaviest rains.

7. Absolutely false! This upsets the ecology of animals and causes them to become dependent on man. Chipmunks, squirrels, and raccoons get used to being

fed and will chew through packs and boxes to get at food. And bears will become bold and downright dangerous!

8. False. Many people take to the backcountry to get away from the trappings of civilization. Your "improvements" may be interpreted by them as full-scale "development"!

9. C. It requires a very hot fire to burn aluminum foil completely. Partially oxidized foil is the scourge of the backcountry. Bottles and cans have been outlawed in many federal wilderness areas because people won't pack them out. Aluminum foil may be next!

10. No way! It's never all right to inflict your noise on others.

11. False. It's unethical, illegal, and it hurts the trees!

12. This is debatable. Purists would say "true," but I disagree. When the woods are drenched from a week-long rain, you need a small axe, saw, and a knife to make fire. First, saw off a 12-inch length of dead log and split it with the axe to get at the dry wood inside. Then slice fine shavings (tinder) from the heartwood and you'll have a roaring fire in no time.

Axes don't damage forests; irresponsible people do! Score your answer correct if you are in philosophical agreement with either viewpoint.

13. C (Purists would disagree.) Bright-colored equipment is essential to the safety of an expedition in remote country. If you float local streams and never make remote trips—and are bothered by bright colors—you may wisely choose earth tones. Otherwise, vivid hues simply make good sense. I don't mind seeing an orange tent or a red canoe. But I do mind litter, noise, and graffiti!

Score your answer correct if you agree philosophically with these viewpoints.

14.   No way! When bacteria attack biodegradable products they reproduce and use up oxygen, which harms fish and aquatic organisms. Just because a product is "biodegradable" doesn't mean it is good for the environment!

15. True! A responsible outdoorsperson *always* packs out his/her trash!

16. C. Many outdoorspeople (myself included) prefer to do all their cooking on a stove. However, it is ethical and legal to build fires in most publicly owned wilderness areas, and that includes sand and gravel bars in navigable rivers. Nonetheless, you are strongly urged to use a stove instead of a fire whenever possible, especially in well-traveled and "ecologically sensitive" areas. No conscientious outdoorsperson would think of making a campfire on delicate vegetation!

Score your answer correct if your heart was in the right place!

17. E. Don't take these responsibilities lightly. You are responsible for any forest fire you cause, and penalties are severe. So make sure your flames are dead out! If you don't know what to bring on a canoe trip, read a book about it before you go. And do help others in trouble and educate everyone you meet about "neglect and the proper way."

18. False. The sound and smell of motors is certainly offensive to many people—the reason why they are banned from some lakes. However, motors do little, if any, damage to lake and river ecosystems.

19. Absolutely false! It is illegal and unethical to cut green trees. Use an air mattress or foam pad; it's more comfortable!

20. True. Whenever possible, use the "honey rather than guns" approach. Most damage to ecosystems is the result of ignorance, not wanton vandalism. People will usually do the "right thing" once they've been properly and patiently educated. Be a spokesperson for the environment. And practice what you teach!

Scoring the Test

Each question is worth one point. A score of 20 is possible.

19-20 ENVIRONMENTAL EXPERT!

17-18 FIRST-CLASS SCOUT

15-16 KNOWLEDGEABLE TENDERFOOT

13-14 FUN-LOVING LOAFER: Sorry, your good times are being had at the expense of the environment!

12 or less BACKCOUNTRY BUMPKIN! You need help. Take someone along who earned a higher score.

INDEX

CANOEING AND CAMPING